Scuba Diving

Scuba Diving

Consultant Editor
Graeme Gourlay

**Eagle
Editions**

AN OCEANA BOOK

Published by Eagle Editions Ltd
11 Heathfield
Royston
Hertfordshire SG8 5BW

ISBN 1-86160-434-3

QUMAISD

This book is produced by
Quantum Publishing Ltd
6 Blundell Street
London N7 9BH

Project Manager: Rebecca Kingsley
Designer: Wayne Humphries

Manufactured in Singapore by
United Graphics

Printed in Singapore by
Star Standard Industries Pte Ltd

CONTENTS

FOREWORD

Earth. Perhaps a more logical name for our planet should be Water. More than seven tenths of the globe's surface is covered by it, and it sustains all life as we know it. Since the beginning of time we have travelled on it, fought wars on it, even played upon its temperamental surface. Yet rarely have we ventured beneath the waves – the occasional foray was attempted in often bizarre contraptions, but the full wonders of this forbidden realm largely remained a mystery.

The invention of the aqualung 50 years ago unlocked the door, Alice-in-Wonderland style. For the first time we could descend with relative ease into what was dubbed by Jacques Cousteau as 'the silent world'. Weightless and amazed, those pioneering sub-aquanauts swam with manta rays, marvelled at coral reefs and were humbled by sharks.

Today millions of people have learned to dive. The basics can be mastered in a few days, and the sport appeals to young and old, male and female – to anyone interested in exploring the sea. You don't have to be super fit, in fact many seriously disabled people gain great pleasure and satisfaction from diving.

Some divers are obsessed by wrecks, others are fascinated by the marine life. A few explore deep and dangerous cave systems, others venture beneath the ice around the poles and many only dive in warm, tropical waters.

Whatever their particular interest, all divers are united by one common bond – the shared experience of swimming freely in our seas. Here is your chance to find out just how easy it is to join them and discover the true wonders of the deep.

1

INTRODUCING SCUBA

The invention of scuba diving equipment has enabled man to leave dry land and discover the secrets deep beneath the oceans. When diving legend Jacques Cousteau and two colleagues invented a way to breathe safely underwater, they changed our perception of the depths for ever.

This chapter traces the history of underwater exploration, from the first dives made by the ancient Greeks and Japanese to the ground breaking invention of scuba diving equipment and the amazing world it revealed.

BELOW: With the invention of self-contained underwater breathing apparatus (SCUBA), divers were given the freedom of the seas

WHAT IS SCUBA?

The invention and development of scuba equipment, or self-contained underwater breathing apparatus as it was first called, and the freedom that it gave people in the water, have transformed many parts of the world into underwater playgrounds for thousands of people. It has also greatly extended our knowledge of this exciting environment, from the warm, blue, tropical waters to those of the cooler regions.

We now know, for example, that the world's largest fish, the exquisitely patterned whale shark, is a harmless plankton-eater. Whales, who punctuate their long voyages by blowing enormous plumes of spray into the air when they breathe, are caring parents. Sharks, once feared by all who used the seas, still have to be treated with respect but now command such interest and concern that people are campaigning for the protection of many species, including even the fearsome great white.

Thousands of pleasure divers take pictures or videos so that they can show their friends and families a glimpse of the world that they find so fascinating. Many also add purpose to their diving by taking part in conservation activities, which help us to

RIGHT: Wrecks make natural playgrounds for scuba divers
BELOW: Under the surface , every colour and shape imaginable!

understand more about the sea and its marine life.

All this followed the development in the 1940s of a device which enabled a diver to breathe safely from a tank of compressed air. It was called a demand valve or regulator because it regulated the supply of air and delivered it as required, or 'on demand', as the diver began to inhale.

Three people were behind that development: two young French naval officers and an engineer trying to devise a way to run cars on coal gas because petrol was rationed in France during World War II. The naval officers were Jacques Cousteau,

who later became a legendary underwater explorer, and Phillipe Taillez, his friend and long-time colleague. Cousteau met the engineer, Emile Gagnan, during a visit to Paris and daringly tried a version of the valve in the river Marne.

Subsequently, in June 1943, at Bandol, on the Mediterranean coast, and watched by his two friends, Cousteau swam down to a depth of 18m (59ft), using an improved version of the valve. He wrote afterwards: 'Now at last we have time to explore the silent world.' Indeed, the world was on the threshold of a new era in exploration, as men and women donned the black-rubber suits and fins of the wartime frogmen to discover more about life in the sea.

The early films of pioneers like Cousteau and Hans Hass and his wife, Lottie, inspired a generation of pleasure divers. Today, people of all ages go diving, from young children in the care of their parents to men and women in their 70s, 80s and even a few in their 90s. They revel in the delight of seeing coral reefs pulsating with life, with vividly coloured fish darting about in a world which is the original cradle of all life on earth, and are lured back into the sea time and time again.

THE FIRST DIVES

When did men first take a huge breath and disappear all too briefly beneath the waves, the salt water stinging their eyes and their lungs bursting while they tried to make out the blurred images which they saw? For millions of years the sea and the world beneath its surface must have seemed an awesome place, inhabited by fearsome monsters and subject to terrifying storms. Yet all the clues point to the first dives having been made in ancient times.

Archaeologists excavating the remains of some early settlements, for example, have found piles of shells which could only have been obtained from the sea, while drawings from the Palaeolithic period show male figures harpooning fish. The ancient Greeks practised military and commercial diving. Homer, in his epic poem *The Iliad*, written centuries before the birth of Christ, described the use of divers in the Trojan War, and Greek laws have been found dating back to the third century BC regulating the activities of those who dived for sunken treasure. The famous Japanese pearl-diving women, the *ama*, have been gathering pearl oysters, shellfish and edible seaweed since before the birth of Christ. Elsewhere in the world, divers have been

Below: Illustration shows the legend of Alexander the Great, in glass diving bell

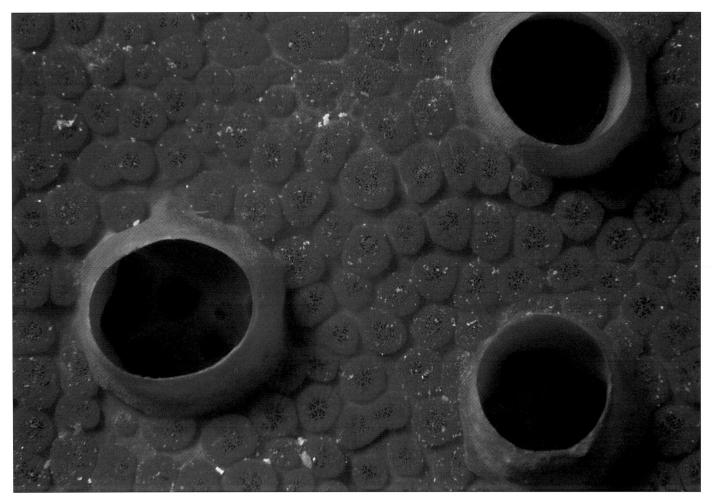

ABOVE: The simple sponge grows in complex shapes beneath quiet reefs

recovering sponges, rare corals and pearls for countless years without special breathing apparatus.

At first, the sea must have been regarded as both a source of food and a means of travel. People must have plunged into the water to retrieve the fish that they had speared and to harvest seaweed and shellfish. When they made rafts and boats, there must have been occasions when, holding their breath, they dived down to repair the vessels or to recover articles which had fallen overboard.

As time went by, curiosity and necessity must have overcome their fears, and some particularly brave souls must have leapt into the sea clutching heavy rocks to overcome their natural buoyancy and so sink deeper. Indeed, this seems to have been one of the earliest techniques used to explore the depths of the sea. In *Divers and Diving,* Reg Vallintine describes how sponge divers went to depths of 22m (72ft) and more to get the best specimens. They filled their mouths and ears with oil and then covered their ears with sponges soaked in oil to counter the effects of water pressure. On reaching the bottom, they spat out some of the oil, ignored the pain in their ears and began

collecting the sponges. When they were ready to return to the surface, they tugged on the rope attached to the heavy rock which had taken them to the bottom and were hauled up.

Vallintine describes many other attempts made by early men to dive to collect coral, valuable items from wrecked ships, during wars. The imperial purple dye from the murex shell which the ancient Greeks used could only have been obtained by diving. The invention of the diving bell – like an inverted drinking glass into which air was pumped – enabled divers to go to greater depths and work underwater for hours at a time.

LEFT: Shells from the shores of Malaysia

THE EARLY DAYS

The first really practical diving bell was devised in 1717 by a British astronomer, Edmund Halley, who is better known for the comet named after him – Halley's Comet – because he was the first person to calculate its orbit. His diving bell was an open-bottomed wooden chamber, with glass windows set into the top to admit light. Casks full of air were connected to the bell with leather tubes. As they were forced lower in the water, the surrounding pressure forced the fresh air into the bell.

The inspiration for the idea came from an air-breathing beetle which brings air bubbles down from the surface on the hairs of its legs to fill the dome-like nest that it has built underwater.

In principle, the diving bells in commercial use today are little different, though much more sophisticated. Air is delivered to them from powerful pumps on the surface and the occupants are also in communication with those monitoring their dive and operating the equipment from above. These modern bells are frequently used as lifts to transport divers from the surface to the seabed or other underwater areas where they are working, such as a shipwreck or the foundations of an oil rig, a bridge or another such structure.

The divers live under pressure for several days at a time in a chamber on the surface, usually on a support ship. The smaller submersible decompression chamber which takes them down or brings them back from the work site is maintained at the same pressure and locks onto the main chamber in such a way that no pressure is lost.

However, back in the 17th century, inventors were struggling to find ways in which to give divers greater freedom. Many different and ingenious ideas were tried, but it was not until early in the 19th century that the first practical diving equipment was devised. An Englishman, Augustus Siebe, whose name still lives on today in connection with diving equipment, especially in the commercial field, produced a diving suit which consisted of a helmet attached to a jacket. Air pumped down from the surface into the helmet kept the water at chin level so that the diver could breathe, but if they stumbled or fell there was a danger that the air would escape and allow water to rush in, with fatal consequences.

Siebe later developed a combined suit and helmet which completely enclosed divers and so gave them greater freedom of movement. This has been refined into the modern standard diving suit, which is in general commercial use today. Made of rugged, rubberised canvas, the one-piece suit has seals at the neck and wrists and is fitted with a brass helmet through which air is pumped to the diver. The helmet is big enough for divers to move their heads about so that they can look out of various windows, and valves enable them to adjust their buoyancy. It is ideal for working in difficult and unpleasant situations, like dirty and polluted water. However, divers have to wear lead-soled boots weighing about 9kg (20lb) each and carry even heavier lead weights slung round their backs and chests to counteract the buoyancy of the suit. There are also one-piece suits, which look much like suits of armour and are made of metal. These enable divers to work at great depths, but the air inside the suits is maintained at the same pressure as on land. This eliminates the risk of divers suffering from the 'bends', the dreaded condition which can strike divers who surface too quickly, before dangerous bubbles of gas have had sufficient time to disperse safely from their systems. All of the joints are articulated so that divers can walk about freely and move their arms, allowing them to perform useful work.

ABOVE: Vibrant colours vie with ancient wrecks in the Red Sea

RIGHT: Early diving involved a large support team on the surface

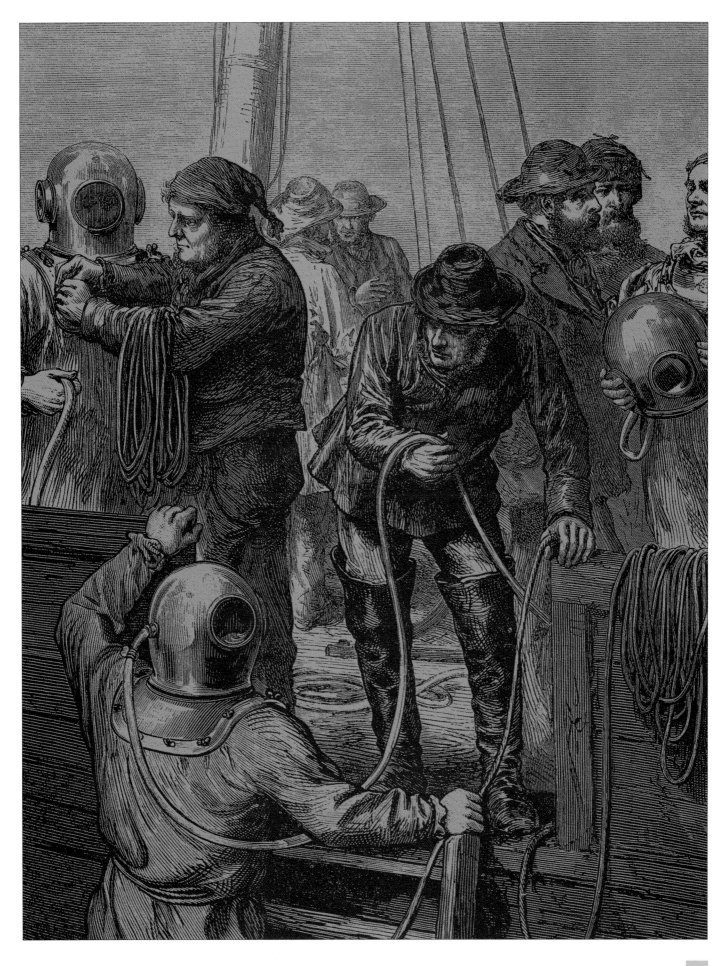

The self-contained breathing apparatus and more flexible wet or dry suit, mask and fins worn by pleasure divers are also used for commercial purposes, because they give greater freedom of movement in many situations. However, full-face masks or light-weight helmets are preferable when working in dirty and polluted waters.

But man is still an insignificant creature when pitted against the sea. The depths to which pleasure divers can sensibly descend are insignificant when compared to the deepest parts of the world's oceans, which average about 3,730m (12,239ft) – nearly eight times greater than the world's tallest buildings. For pleasure diving, most training agencies stipulate a depth limit of 30m (98.5ft). However, by using specialised equipment and specially developed breathing mixtures, commercial divers are able to operate at much greater depths than this, and some have even taken part in underwater living experiments, spending time in 'houses' sunk into the sea.

It is still possible to dive to the remains of one of these experiments, Cousteau's Conshelf II, which is situated on a terrace at a depth of about 12m (39ft) in the Red Sea. The four orange-painted, steel buildings were shipped from Nice, in southern France, to Sudan and then out to Roman Reef, 8km (5 miles) off-shore, in 1963. Some of the buildings were removed after the experiment was completed, but a mushroom-shaped garage for a saucer-shaped midget submarine remains, as well as another structure. Among other tasks, the silver-suited aquanauts spent time observing shark behaviour, but they also studied marine life in general. Space astronauts also train for their missions in huge water tanks, the freedom of diving helping them to get used to the weightlessness of outer space.

A new breed of adventurous pleasure divers – 'technical' divers, or 'techies' – has also begun to venture to much greater depths than the modest 30m (98.5ft) recommended for the majority. Their methods have enabled them to explore three famous wrecks – those of the *Lusitania,* the *Andrea Doria* and the HMHS *Britannic.* The *Lusitania* was sunk off the Irish coast by a German U-boat in 1915. The *Andrea Doria*, which is often described as the 'holy grail' of thrill-seekers, lies at the bottom of the Atlantic at a depth of about 70m (230ft), some 80.5km (50 miles) off Nantucket (USA). The hospital ship HMHS *Britannic* is a World War I shipwreck which is still in surprisingly good condition. It lies on the seabed at a depth of 120m (394ft) in a busy shipping lane in the Mediterranean Sea off Greece. Travel operators have even been offering dives to see the wreck of the

RIGHT: Exploring the delicate undersea coral formations – what a privilege!

Titanic, the famous liner which hit an iceberg and sank in 1912 on her maiden voyage across the Atlantic.

Apart from the highly specialised equipment that they use and the gases that they have to breathe, deep-sea divers have to pay the penalty of decompression times of several hours before it is safe for them to surface.

In order to reach greater depths, scientists and explorers have to resort to special vessels, like the bathyscaph *Trieste,* which reached the deepest part of the ocean, 10,900m (35,761ft), in 1958, and other submersibles and remotely operated vehicles which have their own lights and cameras.

Despite all this activity, so much of our planet is covered by water that exciting discoveries continue to be made, not only by scientists and marine biologists but also by pleasure divers.

BELOW: Only those who peep below the surface will ever glimpse such beauty

2

IS SCUBA FOR ME?

Today, scuba diving is one of the fastest-growing recreational sports world-wide, with millions of active divers and many well-established training programmes. No longer is diving regarded as an exclusive club, open only to those in peak physical condition. Indeed, it is recognised that, with proper training and a healthy respect for the underwater environment, diving can be a safe and enjoyable pastime for many people.

Scuba diving offers a fantastic opportunity to explore the wonders of the world's oceans, but can, at times, be a demanding sport. Always remember that responsible divers seek proper training and ensure that they are prepared for the diving that they intend to pursue.

This chapter will help you to choose who to learn with and enable you to prepare for a diving course. It also provides a ready-reference guide to the important scientific and medical aspects of diving.

BELOW: You never forget your first dive!

FITNESS TO DIVE

GENERAL POINTS

Although scuba diving is a recreational activity for most of us, it is important to remember the potential dangers, to be aware of personal limitations and to keep healthy in body and mind. Remaining rested prior to diving, eating well and not smoking or using recreational drugs or drinking heavily will contribute to good personal health.

Cold or infection, depending on what area is affected and to what extent, may be a temporary disqualifying factor. Exercising regularly should help to maintain personal fitness.

AGE RESTRICTIONS

While there is no single world-wide agreement on the minimum age recommended for scuba diving, most agencies will train divers of 12 years and above. This age assumes that a reasonable level of physical and mental maturity has been reached.

There is usually no upper age limit for candidates wishing to undertake a recreational diving course, although most training agencies recommend regular medicals to monitor both heart and lungs beyond a certain age. Assuming medical fitness, older people may continue diving on a self-assessment basis.

WEIGHT

There is no rule restricting anyone over a certain weight, who is in good medical health, from diving. Training agencies do, however, recommend that divers be aware of their optimum weights and aim to stay as close to them as possible. An overweight recreational diver may be advised to lose weight if he or she becomes out of breath when performing simple tasks.

As fatty tissue absorbs a high volume of nitrogen (approximately five times more than connective tissue), which is also eliminated slowly, an overweight diver is more likely to experience the problems caused when ascending from a dive with high levels of nitrogen still present in the body's tissues (see *Decompression sickness*, p. 31).

ENT

Divers require clear and healthy ears, noses and throats (ENTs) in order to make the necessary adjustments for pressure changes when descending or ascending in water. Diving with a cold that has caused blocked sinuses may either restrict a diver from 'equalising' pressure on the way down or, in some cases, trap air inside the sinuses on the way up. Both situations are very painful and can cause irreversible damage. Permanent or recurring, chronic problems would almost certainly be disqualifying factors for diving.

Decongestants are used by divers to clear blocked sinuses. However, it is best to check with a doctor who is familiar with diving about which are the best to use. Any side effects, such as dizziness or drowsiness, are dangerous when planning to dive. Assuming that no obstructions to the airways are present, deafness need not be a disqualifying factor.

FEMALE DIVERS

It is now agreed that, with the exception of periods of pregnancy, women are not at any greater risk when scuba diving than men. Although it is generally true that women have a lower aerobic capacity than men, by diving sensibly within predetermined, personal limits they can avoid strenuous conditions. Despite some experts' suggestions that women's risk of developing decompression sickness is larger than men's, due to their greater percentage of body fat, studies have provided inconsistent results.

Diving during menstruation or while taking the pill (check with your doctor) is alright unless side effects are experienced. Women should not dive when pregnant because the effect on the unborn child is not known.

ASTHMATICS

There is no simple answer to the question of whether asthmatics are safe to dive. It is unfortunate that asthma or other breathing conditions may preclude any possibility of learning to dive.

During asthma attacks, patients develop partially obstructed airways. The degree of obstruction dictates the severity of the attack. As a diver's airways must remain clear to allow natural pressure changes to occur during descent and ascent, and as many asthmatic attacks are unpredictable, physicians tend to rule out diving.

The use of compressed air in scuba tanks, and the increase of air density when it is breathed at depth, coupled with an increased work rate, may be an eliminating factor for asthmatics whose symptoms are triggered by cold or exercise.

It is possible that those with allergic asthma may be safe to dive, if they have clearly defined triggers that are unlikely to develop under water. There are, in fact, many asthmatics diving today, and statistics suggest they are at no greater risk than other divers.

DIABETES AND EPILEPSY

Both diabetes and epilepsy may be disqualifying factors. Typically, insulin-dependant diabetics and those experiencing regular epileptic seizures are most at risk under water. However, the decision of who may or may not dive is ultimately the responsibility of the patient and the physician.

PHYSICAL DISABILITY

There are many divers with physical disabilities world-wide. Divers with disabilities often describe being underwater as the only time that they are able to move with minimal effort and assistance. Special training agencies offering proper facilities and highly experienced instructors exist for those who want to learn to dive.

MEDICALS

Several methods exist for checking medical fitness to dive. While some training bodies still require a sports-diving medical to be carried out on a regular basis, others use 'yes' or 'no' questionnaires for their students.

Anyone going diving for the first time should consider having a sports-diving medical as it is impossible to review all the possible disqualifying factors here. The medical can be carried out by local physicians, although consulting a doctor with some experience of scuba diving ensures a thorough check-up, including an X-ray of the chest (heart and lungs) and breathing and sinus tests.

Medical questionnaires should be issued and completed prior to commencing a diving course to allow time for examination, should it be required. Misleading information on a medical questionnaire is dangerous, so always be honest.

ABOVE: Once qualified, you are free to explore the seas

COURSES

All entry-level diving courses can be divided into three sections: academic/classroom sessions, confined-water sessions (usually in a swimming pool) and open-water sessions (in coastal waters, lakes, rivers or quarries). Each section is directly related to the next, so a technique will be discussed in the classroom, practised in confined water and demonstrated for assessment in open water. The skills learned on an entry-level course may vary quite dramatically, depending on the training agency. However, all will provide the necessary grounding for safe, enjoyable diving.

ACADEMIC SESSIONS

Prior to entering the water for the first time, it is important to understand fully the basics of scuba diving. Classroom sessions enable formal introductions to be made and the opportunity to check through questionnaires or medical certificates from doctors. Course manuals, videos and other teaching aids, such as overhead projectors, may be used to assist learning.

Academic sessions are typically informal, with instructors encouraging questions to be raised at any time. Essential topics such as the diving environment, diving equipment and the relevance of pressure in diving should be discussed early on in the course. These sessions also provide the first opportunity to see a fully working set of scuba equipment.

At the end of each academic session there may be a quiz or a question-and-answer session. A final test ensures that a good level of information has been retained.

CONFINED-WATER SESSIONS

Once an adequate understanding has been reached for the relevant topics, students are ready to enter the water for the first time using scuba equipment. Entry-level courses do not require that all academic topics have been covered before the first confined-water session. Controlled environments, such as swimming pools, are used to ensure the highest levels of safety.

All training bodies assign a set number of students to each instructor to ensure that each student is closely monitored. Certified instructional assistants may also be in the water to provide support. Skills like mask flooding and clearing, regulator removal and replacement and hovering in mid-water are made easy when demonstrated in steps by an instructor.

OPEN-WATER SESSIONS

Divers never forget their first open-water diving experiences. Initial dives are restricted to shallow depths for safety while students adjust to the unfamiliar environment. Instructors should plan dives in class, discussing chosen routes and things that may be encountered along the way. Each dive offers the opportunity to demonstrate one's understanding of, and ability to perform, skills learned in confined-water sessions. It is important to master skills performed at the surface, as well as those under water, as soon as possible.

At the end of every dive a debriefing session, followed by recording or 'logging' the dive, ensures that everyone receives maximum learning opportunities. Open-water diving environments can vary, and all training agencies strongly recommend that divers do not attempt dives in new environments without the supervision of an experienced diving partner or buddy.

REFERRALS

Most training agencies offer the option of completing an entry-level dive course on a referral basis. Log books are used for recording the completion of each section of the course. Students may then stop training at a pre-determined point for a limited amount of time (usually students complete academic and pool training and then have six months to a year to finish the course). This allows the student not only to complete the course at a later date but also with a different instructor and possibly even in another country (those living near uninviting coastal waters may travel to warm, clear sites to finish the open-water dives).

SCHOOL OR CLUB?

Both schools and clubs will use the academic/confined-/open-water system of education.

DIVE SCHOOLS

The school system tends to be a quicker method of learning to dive. Typically, training is undertaken in blocks, so a course might run over one week or several weekends. Dive schools are businesses, so instructors work on a part- or full-time basis. They are diving professionals as they rely on teaching for at least part of their income. However, the word 'professional' does not imply that they are more skilled or experienced than instructors working under a club system. Schools are not, on the whole, run to provide diving opportunities beyond training.

DIVE CLUBS

The club system offers an alternative to the school system and the chance to enter into a new and exciting social network. Clubs tend to suit those who have little opportunity to take time

ABOVE: Swimming pools also offer a perfect environment to practice snorkelling techniques

out from work. They offer tuition in sessions of several hours at a time on, for example, a once-a-week basis in the evening. For this reason, club courses are usually more drawn-out. Beyond training, divers have the chance to meet other members and to arrange pleasure dives through the club.

TRAINING AGENCIES

There are many recognised scuba diving training agencies worldwide. Each has developed its own course structure and individuality. When choosing which agency to learn to dive with, it is important to ignore comments from those with extreme biases and to consider the following points:

1. *Choose to learn through a system that suits your individual needs.*
2. *Make sure that the agency you choose is recognised at your intended dive destination – not all are.*
3. *All training agencies meet required standards. Choose a good instructor – who will influence your learning and skill development – perhaps by recommendation.*
4. *Make sure that your training centre's equipment looks well maintained and fits well.*

CONTINUING EDUCATION

Entry-level scuba diving courses are only intended to give you basic knowledge and experience. All agencies recommend that further training be sought to increase this level. Learning new skills and fine-tuning old ones is part of becoming a well-rounded diver. It is important not to rush too quickly through to the higher grades. Experience, not qualifications, builds confidence, awareness and ability under water.

Continuing education offers you the opportunity to become a better dive buddy by learning how to search for, lift to the surface and rescue a diver requiring assistance. First-aid procedures, such as in-water artificial ventilation (AV), treatment for shock, monitoring a patient's vital signs and administering oxygen as a treatment for diving injuries, may either be learnt in stages (a bit in each course) or in a single course. Advanced courses enable you to learn leadership skills. Planning and leading dives, managing diving emergencies and supervising students in training all require high levels of skill and experience.

RIGHT: Ensuring they have the right equipment for the task in hand leaves these divers free to enjoy their dive in safety

PHYSICS OF DIVING

LIGHT

Much of the sun's natural light is reflected off the water's surface, resulting in low light levels under water. Unfortunately for divers, the level of the light that does filter down through the water is reduced further still by other elements.

Light travel (distance and direction) is affected by the density of the matter through which it passes. In air, light travels relatively undisturbed, but with the increased density of water natural light is diffused quickly and absorbed and so travels a comparably short distance.

The density of a body of water is also affected by any particles suspended in it. This is referred to as the turbidity of the water and may change in the same area from one day to the next. The more turbid the water the faster light will be diffused as it travels down, resulting in lower levels of light at shallower depths. During the day, most diving can be carried out without the use of torches.

The most noticeable effect of low light levels is that colours are filtered out as you descend. Red is the first colour to be lost at shallow depths where surrounding light levels are still high. Blues and greens will still be present at great depths where surrounding light levels are low (see the Colour change diagram). Colours can be easily restored by the use of a dive light.

The direction that light travels in is also affected by water. The change of direction that light takes when moving from air to water, or from water to air, is known as 'refraction'. The effect of refraction under water causes objects to appear nearer and larger than they really are by approximately 20 to 25 per cent.

COLOUR CHANGE

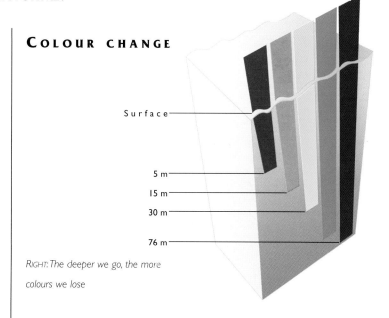

RIGHT: The deeper we go, the more colours we lose

This phenomenon may be clearly observed by placing a solid object, such as a pencil, halfway into a clear glass filled with water. In the water the pencil is magnified. Divers experience this as light passes from the water into the air space inside a mask.

HEAT

Water conducts heat away from the body approximately 20 times faster than air. Heat conduction is the process that transmits heat via direct contact. Water also has a very high heat capacity and can absorb thousands of times more heat than air.

It is important for divers' safety that the heat lost into the surrounding water is kept to a minimum. The colder the water

BELOW: The water always wins! Dress for the deepest (and coldest) part of your dive

HEAT LOSS

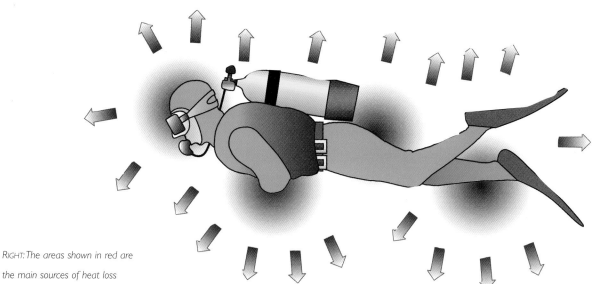

RIGHT: The areas shown in red are the main sources of heat loss

the faster it will conduct heat away from the body. However, exposure in any temperature of water may result in heat levels becoming dangerously low and a diver becoming hypothermic.

Hypothermia (conditon of subnormal body temperature) is a very real problem for divers. In fact, most divers will, without realising it, have experienced mild hypothermia on a dive. In extreme cases hypothermia can be very serious and even fatal. Typically, a hypothermic diver will shake visibly and uncontrollably. In this situation it is vital that heat loss is halted quickly by exiting the water and raising the body temperature. To minimise heat loss, divers wear protective suits which provide them with an extra layer of warmth.

SOUND

Unlike light, sound carries further in water than in air. Sound waves must pass from one molecule to another, so they travel quickly in dense matter where the molecules are close together. Under water, this equates to sound travelling approximately four times faster than in air, resulting in it reaching further. For this reason, sound is used for communication between divers or even from the surface to the diver.

The human brain determines the direction from which a sound is coming by the time it takes to travel from one ear to the other, as well as by the relative intensity. Under water, a sound may reach both ears in quick succession and at almost identical levels of intensity, making it very difficult to determine its direction of origin.

SOUND PERSPECTIVE

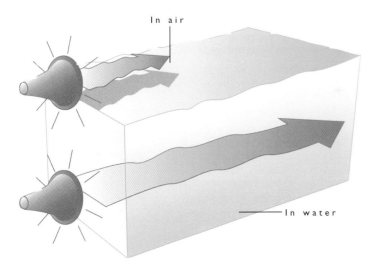

In air

In water

ABOVE: You can't depend on your ears for sound-direction under water

ABOVE: It is important to practise buoyancy control in a swimming pool first

BUOYANCY

Learning and maintaining good buoyancy-control skills is one of the primary objectives of all divers. To achieve this, it is first necessary to understand what buoyancy is.

Buoyancy refers to the tendency of any solid object either to float or sink. The characteristics of buoyancy were first observed by Archimedes before 200 BC. He discovered that an object would float if it displaced a weight of water greater than its own and would sink if it displaced less.

Any object that floats on top of water is referred to as positively buoyant; one that sinks is correspondingly negatively buoyant. There is also one other state of buoyancy that divers especially are aware of. When an object neither floats nor sinks it is referred to as neutrally buoyant. Gaining neutral buoyancy under water allows divers freedom to move in any direction with minimum effort.

As the weight of salt water is slightly greater than that of fresh water, an object must displace a smaller amount of salt water to be positively buoyant. Therefore the same object may float in salt water but be neutral or sink in fresh water.

All entry-level courses include buoyancy skills and techniques as standard. Beyond these courses, however, divers may develop their skills through workshops or by using such proven systems as the BTSI Diamond Reef Hover stations.

PRESSURE

Although air pressure surrounds us all the time, we are very rarely aware of it. At sea level, the force exerted on us is the weight of the earth's atmosphere. This may vary slightly with changes in weather, but is generally measured as a constant of one atmosphere (atmospheric pressure) or one bar (barometric pressure). Divers often measure pressure in bar or pounds per square inch (psi); one bar is equal to 14.7psi. Ascending above sea level, for example when flying, reduces atmospheric pressure to less than one atmosphere.

The increased weight of water means that pressure increases occur rapidly, so that at just 10m (33ft) below the surface the total pressure has doubled to two atmospheres (one atmosphere of air pressure and one atmosphere of water pressure).

The surrounding pressure on land or under water is referred to as ambient pressure. Ambient pressure will continue to increase at a rate of one atmosphere for every additional 10m (33ft).

DIVING GAUGES AND ABSOLUTE PRESSURES

Diving gauges used to measure pressures greater than one atmosphere are usually set up so that atmospheric pressure is marked as zero. Any reading taken underwater is then a gauge pressure. Adding atmospheric pressure to a gauge reading gives total or absolute pressure.

THE COMPOSITION OF AIR

The air that we breathe is made up of a mixture of gases. The inhaled oxygen content in air is 21 per cent, though much of this is replaced by carbon dioxide at the exhalation phase. Nitrogen is the largest inert gas at 78 per cent, while a final one per cent is made up of other inert gases. Most diving manuals include other inert gases with nitrogen and list them as a total of 79 per cent. Whether at atmospheric pressure of one bar or when compressed in a diving cylinder to extreme pressures of 300 bar, the percentages of each gas in the air remain the same.

BOYLE'S LAW (GAS PRESSURE, VOLUME AND DENSITY RELATIONSHIPS)

Assuming constant temperature, Boyle's law states that changes in pressure will have a direct affect on both the volume and density of a gas. It also observes that these changes will be relative to each other. So, for example, an open-ended container full of air at the surface will, at 10m (33ft), have halved in volume and doubled in density. Higher ambient pressures present at greater depths will continue to lower air volume and increase air density. For divers, this affects such bodily air spaces as the lungs and sinuses.

DALTON'S LAW (PARTIAL PRESSURES OF GASES)

Dalton's law states that the total pressure of a gas mixture is equal to the individual pressure of each of the gases within the mixture added together. These individual pressures are known as partial pressures and may also be present when dissolved in a liquid such as blood or in body tissue. At one bar (atmospheric pressure), the partial pressure of each gas in air is: oxygen 0.21 bar, nitrogen 0.78 bar, other inert gases 0.1 bar.

The human body is regulated to deal efficiently at atmospheric pressure with each of the gases that we breathe in air. With these laws in mind, it is possible to determine the partial pressure of any gas when breathed at depth. At 10m (33ft), with a full lung volume, the density of air will have doubled, so the partial pressure of oxygen will be 0.42 bar, nitrogen 1.56 bar and other inert gases 0.2 bar – a total of two bar.

In other words, divers continually breathe strong levels of nitrogen and oxygen, making it possible to overload themselves with either gas. This can have damaging side effects.

RIGHT: A different set of physical laws applies beneath the surface

PHYSIOLOGY OF DIVING

BAROTRAUMA (PRESSURE-RELATED INJURY)

Physical injury to any part of the body caused by unequal air pressure is called 'barotrauma'. Injury is caused by either the compression or expansion of a body part. For divers who experience continual pressure changes when descending or ascending, barotrauma is potentially serious. Problems typically manifest themselves in the ears and sinuses as the pressure increases, and in the lungs as pressure decreases.

Most commonly, divers experience a 'squeeze' in the middle ear upon descent as pressure inside the sinuses increases and the middle-ear pressure remains constant. Unless this pressure differential is actively equalised, barotrauma occurs. While for a lucky few this pressure change happens naturally, most divers have to perform the Valsalva manoeuvre every metre or so – pinching the nose and gently blowing forces air into the middle ear. On ascent, the middle ear should naturally release air into the sinuses, although it is possible to experience a 'reverse block'. This is why it is unwise to dive with a heavy cold.

Damage to the lungs caused by unequal air pressure is called pulmonary barotrauma. Alongside decompression sickness, this poses the greatest threat to an ascending diver. Extreme cases can be fatal, so divers are taught to breathe continuously, allowing lung and ambient pressures to remain the same.

In severe cases a lung may burst, but lesser pressures can also cause permanent damage due to overstretching; this may occur when ascending to the surface from just a few metres. A diver with pulmonary barotrauma may experience an arterial gas embolism (AGE). This is the most dangerous pressure-related injury, accounting for a large percentage of diving fatalities. AGE is caused when massive pressure within the lungs forces air to enter the arteries, thus causing a blockages. This may then lead to brain damage due to restricted oxygen levels or a heart attack due to blocked coronary arteries.

OXYGEN TOXICITY

While high levels of oxygen can be metabolised, beyond a certain pressure divers run the risk of inhaling too much and developing oxygen toxicity. Recreational divers breathing in air are at little risk, however, due to maximum-depth restrictions and short dive

LEFT: Wreck exploration is addictive – but watch your depth and time!

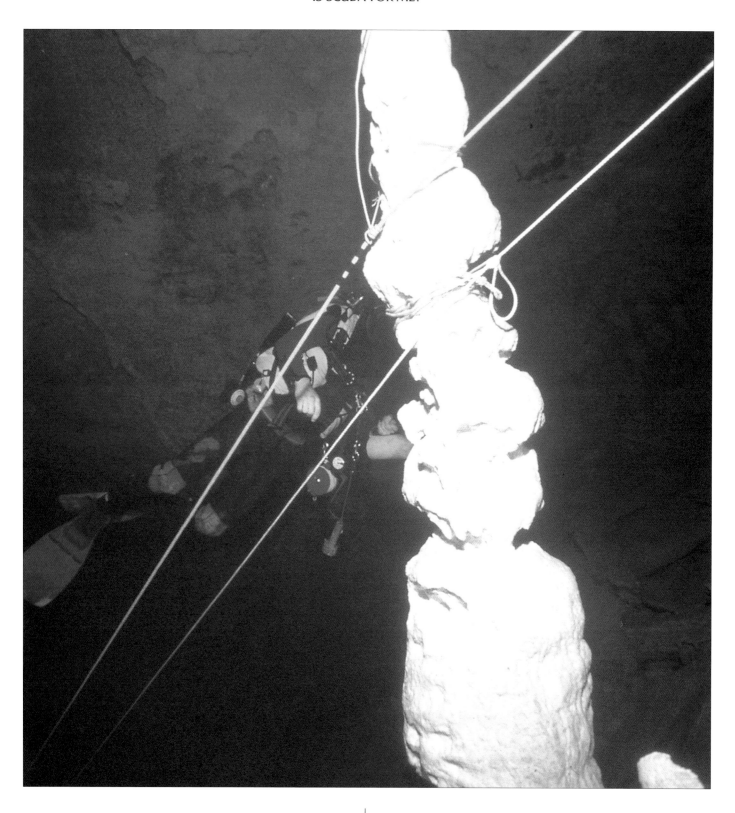

ABOVE: Caves, like wrecks, offer dives with an overhead environment

times. At greater depths, or when breathing a gas mix of oxygen higher than 21 per cent, toxicity becomes a very real hazard.

NITROGEN NARCOSIS

Nitrogen narcosis is a phenomenon that occurs when breathing high pressures of nitrogen. The increased density of the gas as it is inhaled has an anaesthetic quality, causing a feeling of intoxica-

tion. Some divers are more prone to experiencing it than others, but typically narcosis begins to manifest itself between 30 and 40m (98.4 and 131ft). It is possible to build up tolerance levels, allowing higher pressures to be reached than before. While a diver experiencing narcosis is in no medical danger, the side effects may cause irrational thoughts, leading to hazardous behaviour. Removing vital equipment, ignoring signals from dive buddies and failing to monitor time or depth, are some typical examples. As nitrogen narcosis is a problem related only to depth, it can be cured simply by ascending.

DECOMPRESSION SICKNESS

Decompression sickness (DCS), although caused by nitrogen, is not linked to narcosis. It is important to make this distinction and to recognise DCS as a medical condition which, if encountered, requires immediate attention.

DCS is caused when ascending, as nitrogen in the body's tissues exits, either dissolved in the blood or in bubbles. The dissolved state is harmless, but bubbles can compress nerves and/or block circulation. Since bubble formation is in part related to the total amount of nitrogen in the tissues, it is possible to predict safe diving limits. Very long, shallow dives will result in unsafe levels of dissolved nitrogen in the tissues; short, deep dives will have a similar effect. For this reason all recreational diver-training agencies impose maximum depth and time limits to minimise the risk.

The symptoms and severity of DCS may vary, depending on several elements. The size of the bubbles and where they lodge are the greatest determining factors. Through testing, many divers have been found to have small, 'silent' bubbles and yet display no symptoms at all. DCS occurs when ambient pressure

BELOW: Breathing compressed air needs training and careful management

decreases at such a rate that high amounts of dissolved nitrogen form large bubbles, probably by the coalescence of many smaller ones, within the tissues and circulatory system.

DCS may be divided into two categories: DCS type one is less severe, causing joint and limb pains and skin problems. It is from type one that the term 'the bends' comes. In the bends, the blockage of the blood flow to the joints caused by bubbles that have formed around the joints can cause pain and a tendency to keep the limbs bent; hence the name. DCS type two may include such serious manifestations as pulmonary, central-nervous-system and cardiovascular problems.

To avoid DCS when exceeding limits beyond which it is safe to make a direct ascent to the surface, divers make mandatory decompression stops: deliberate, timed stops at a fixed depth, allowing excess nitrogen to leave the body's tissues at a safe rate. In some cases, more than one stop may be required at different depths.

To calculate dive time and depth limits divers should use special tables or a computer. Training on the use of dive tables is given on all entry level diving courses.

BELOW: Illuminated by torchlight, coral at depth reveals its beauty

3

EQUIPMENT

Scuba diving is only possible with the use of highly specialised equipment which allows you to breathe underwater. It is essential to have the correct tools when you dive underwater, and to fully understand their uses and how they work.

Finding the right equipment is just as important as learning the correct techniques. This will enable you to enjoy your diving experience as much as possible, as safely as possible.

This chapter examines the broad range of tools and equipment available to scuba divers, from fins and masks to regulators and gauges.

BELOW: Scuba diving is a great way to relax — to rush is wrong!

DIVING MASKS

The human eye is designed to focus only in the air. In order to enable it to focus under water it is necessary to provide an air space. This is what a diving mask does.

A diving mask also encloses the nose. The reason why ordinary swimming goggles aren't suitable for diving is that increasing pressure during descent cannot be equalised and any water that gets past the seal cannot be evacuated. By enclosing the nose, the diver can simply exhale through the mask to equalise pressure and force water out of the mask.

The mask consists of a glass face plate, a soft neoprene or silicone skirt and an adjustable strap. Tempered or safety glass is used rather than plastic, which scratches easily, or ordinary glass, which can shatter. A nose pocket or finger wells provide access to the nose to allow blocking for ear-clearing.

Some masks have a simple drain or purge valve to help evacuate any water that penetrates past the seal. Most masks have a second or double seal around the mask skirt to help reduce leakage.

A soft skirt helps the mask to match the contours of the face, improving the seal. Neoprene rubber is cheaper, but silicone is usually softer, lasts much longer and is hypo-allergenic. Many divers prefer a clear or translucent skirt as it is less claustrophobic and makes it easier to light models' faces in photographs. Underwater photographers often choose black skirts that block the extraneous light that can impair looking through a camera's view finder. Masks come in different volumes. The lower the volume, the lower the internal space in the mask. By reducing this space, less air is needed to equalise the mask or clear it of water. This is more of a concern to a free diver, who dives on only a single lungful of air, than to a scuba diver whose air supply is virtually unlimited. Low-volume masks are an advantage to photographers

BELOW AND RIGHT: Select your mask with care; it must fit snugly

because the face plate is brought nearer to their eye, enabling them to see small camera view finders more easily.

Straps are designed to span the back of the head for comfort and security. Some use a split-strap design, others a cup. The cup design can be more comfortable if you have long hair and don't use a hood, as it avoids entanglement. Most masks have buckles that permit easy single-handed adjustment, even under water.

For commercial, technical sports diving and specialised polluted or cold-water diving, full-face masks are sometimes used. These enclose both the mouth and nose and often have built-in regulators. Full-face masks require additional training by an approved FFM instructor.

Before use, a new mask should have toothpaste rubbed over the glass. Toothpaste is mildly abrasive and removes agents used in mask manufacturing. If these agents are not removed it will be difficult to stop the mask from fogging up. After this, simply coating the glass with saliva or a commercially available defogging agent and then rinsing it before each dive will prevent misting.

FITTING A MASK

To check a mask for fit, look up slightly and place the mask against your face gently. Don't use the strap. The skirt should make contact with your face all around its seal. Sniff in slightly through your nose, with your mouth closed. The mask should stay in place as you lower your head. If it falls off, or you have to suck in hard, it isn't sealing properly and will be a poor fit under the water – try another. It is a good idea to do this test with a snorkel in your mouth, as gripping the mouthpiece will alter your face and may disturb the mask seal along the sides of your face and just above your upper lip.

VISION

If your eyesight is imperfect you may want to consider a corrected face mask. Many masks can be fitted with off-the-rack

lenses for correcting simple prescription problems. These lenses replace the normal mask glass and can be quickly and easily exchanged if your eyesight alters. More complex prescriptions, including bifocals, can be handled by having custom-built lenses bonded into the mask. Contact lenses can be used, provided that they allow gas exchange to take place; eye bends can result if they do not. Care must be taken that lenses are not lost if your mask is flooded during training or by accident. Consult your instructor or optician for advice on eyesight correction.

SNORKELS

Snorkels allow divers to swim at the surface with their faces submerged without having to lift their heads every few seconds to breathe. Scuba divers use snorkels to swim to and from dive sites on the surface to conserve air and dive-time limits. They can also be used for advanced resuscitation during rescues.

The simplest snorkel is just an open-ended tube with a mouthpiece and a clip to the mask strap. With a little practice and the right techniques, they are very easy to clear of any water that may enter during a breath-hold dive. Snorkels with a wide bore are easiest to breathe through, but are more difficult to clear. Snorkels sometimes use valves to prevent water entering or to make clearing the snorkel easier, especially for beginners.

If you will be snorkelling for a long time, it is vital that the mouthpiece is comfortable. Soft mouthpieces and swivels that let you orientate the mouthpiece in a way that is the best for you are good investments.

Reflective tape on the snorkel's tip makes it easier for your companion or boat and water-toy users to see and avoid you.

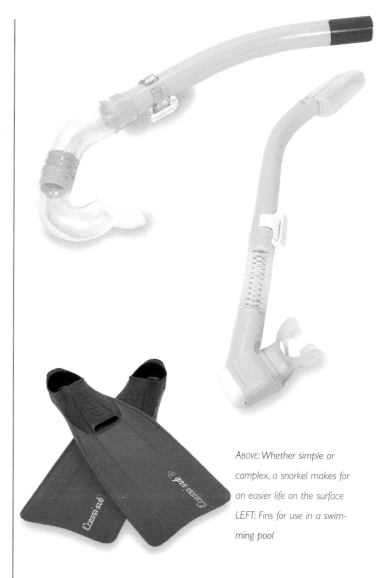

ABOVE: Whether simple or complex, a snorkel makes for an easier life on the surface
LEFT: Fins for use in a swimming pool

BELOW: Most divers carry a snorkel for surface swims

FINS

Fins are designed to propel divers through the water and to increase their mobility. Humans swim inefficiently compared to fish and marine mammals, especially when encumbered by scuba equipment. Swimmers also use strokes that churn the water and can frighten marine life. Using fins requires much less effort, reducing exertion and prolonging the gas supply, and allows the diver to cut cleanly and smoothly through the water. This is less disturbing to animals, making them much more approachable.

Fins are available in different styles to suit such different purposes as casual snorkelling, scuba diving and competitive free diving. The main differences are in the length and rigidity of the blades. For casual snorkelling, which is often undertaken by people who are not 'dive fit' or youngsters whose leg muscles are not fully formed, small, flexible blades are usually best. Snorkellers tend to spend most of their time at the surface and use a shallow kick. Because the blades only work when they are submerged, a fin tip that breaks the surface contributes nothing to the swimmer's propulsion.

Scuba divers are normally fully submerged and can use a much wider kicking action. To propel themselves through the water while wearing bulky equipment, larger, stiffer blades are used.

Competitive free divers use long, narrow fins designed to send them the maximum distance with the absolute minimum of effort in order to conserve precious oxygen, which is most rapidly consumed through finning. These fins are most effective when fully submerged. Competitive free divers are usually very well conditioned and are comfortable with these specialised fins.

BELOW: Fins for use in open water

Using modern composites and polymers allows the blade to flex optimally to suit the type of diving and strength of the user. Fins are designed to deliver the most thrust on the down stroke or 'power stroke'. During the recovery kick, they are designed to minimise effort. The shape of the fin, the use of vents and the rigidity of the blade all contribute to a fin's performance.

The blade is attached to a moulded foot pocket. Open-back fins are normally used with hard-sole boots and are secured using adjustable straps. Full-foot fins fit like a slipper and are used either with bare feet or with a wet-suit sock. They are sized like shoes.

Hard-sole boots with open-back fins are most appropriate for beach diving over rocky or stony shore lines or in cold water, where the boot adds thermal protection. Slip-on fins are best suited to sandy beaches and diving from boats in warmer waters, where thermal protection is less important.

Composite plastics and rubbers are often used to provide the maximum performance in the blade and the greatest comfort in the foot pocket.

Fins are designed to provide momentum, not lift. The key to a proper finning technique is neutral buoyancy and proper trim, usually horizontal. Proper fin control is essential to avoid damaging coral, disturbing visibility or becoming entangled in guide lines.

REGULATORS

Regulators are at the heart of self-contained diving. Prior to their invention, air was either pumped from the surface, which required a restrictive hose, or divers had to turn the air in their tanks on and off manually to breathe. Regulators do this automatically, supplying only as much air as is needed.

Regulators drop the pressure in two stages. The first stage attaches to the tank and reduces the cylinder pressure, which falls throughout the dive, to a steady nine or ten bars above the surrounding water pressure. A flexible, single hose links the first stage to the second stage, which is held in the diver's mouth. Air supplied at nine or ten bars to the second stage is then reduced to the exact pressure of the surrounding water. Valves in the first and second stages open to let air flow to the diver and close to conserve air when the diver stops inhaling. The diver's lungs act like a switch, providing the signal to turn the air supply on and off.

First stages can be unbalanced or balanced. Unbalanced regulators do not perform as well as balanced regulators at depth, under high demand or at low tank pressures. They are less expensive to buy and to maintain. As tank pressure falls, breathing may become noticeably more difficult and so provide a warning that the diver is getting low on air.

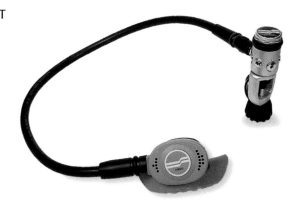

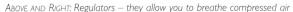

ABOVE AND RIGHT: Regulators – they allow you to breathe compressed air

Balanced regulators provide easier breathing at depth and when under high demand, such as when fighting a current or sharing air using a safe second (see *Alternative air sources,* p. 38). They perform consistently until the cylinder is nearly empty, providing virtually no warning of the air running low.

Piston- or diaphragm-operated first stages are available. Neither has a definitive advantage over the other.

Outlets on the first stage allow such accessories as safe seconds, BCD and dry-suit inflators, tools and pressure gauges or computers to be attached.

Second stages are available in several different designs. Most offer features to make breathing easier. Inhaling is separated into two distinct phases. The initial phase of the inhalation has to open a valve in the second stage to begin the air flow. This is usually held closed by a small spring. Once this valve opens, the flow of air has to be maintained at a sufficient rate for divers to get as much air as they need with the minimum of effort.

To breathe in, a diaphragm built into the second stage must be collapsed. As it collapses, it depresses a lever that in turn opens a valve that seals off the air supply from the first stage and tank. To minimise the effort needed to open this valve, known as cracking, some second stages are pneumatically balanced. They use a combination of the spring and air pressure to close the valve. Because the air does some of the work, a less resistant spring is used, requiring less energy from the diver's lungs to open. Others are servo-assisted and use a pilot-valve design instead. These use two valves: a smaller one is opened by the diver's inhalation; the first valve then opens the second, larger, main valve without further effort by the diver.

So that the diver does not have to suck hard to keep the air flowing once the valve has been opened, ventures are usually used. These channel some of the air to create a vacuum. This vacuum helps to keep the diaphragm depressed without further effort from the diver.

Some second stages have user-operated controls to allow the adjustment of the cracking effort or the venturi. This can reduce free flow when the regulator is out of the mouth or when swimming against a current or riding a DPV.

Regulators are designed to be fail-safe. This means that if a spring were to fai, the regulator would lock open rather than close off the air supply to the diver. This causes a free flow which is easy to breathe from. It is a skill that is taught in most entry-level diving classes.

For diving in very cold conditions, specially adapted regulators are useful. Air entering the regulator is significantly cooler than it is in the tank as pressure drops in the first and second stages. Any moisture in the air can freeze, causing icing inside the regulator and creating a free flow or possibly an air failure. Water in contact with the first- and second-stage external parts can also cause problems. Air chambers, silicone grease, non-slip surfaces, heat sinks and isolation diaphragms are just some regulator modifications that are used to combat icing.

Many recreational divers use nitrox rather than normal air for diving. Technical divers also often use nitrox, eliox, trimix and pure oxygen for breathing at different depths. Whenever anything other than normal air is used with a regulator, you must ensure that the regulator is suitable or can be made so. The risk of explosion or fire is very real if incompatible regulators are used with gases containing higher than normal oxygen percentages.

Both cold-water diving and the use of nitrox or other gases require specialised training beyond entry level.

BELOW: Some regulators have exhaust valves on the side

ALTERNATIVE AIR SOURCES

Although techniques are taught to help a diver who has either run out of air, or has experienced a failure of the breathing system under water, to escape to the surface, this is not always easy or even possible. This is especially true of deep dives, dives into shipwrecks or caves or those under an icecap. To minimise the risk of air failure and maximise the ease with which this can be handled if it does occur, most divers carry an alternative air source.

Alternative air sources may be buddy-dependent or self-sufficient. Buddy-dependent systems are there to help partners: if they run out of air they can breathe from your tank using an octopus or safe second. This is usually a spare second-stage regulator attached to your regulator first stage which is often combined with the BCD inflator to save space. If you run out of air, you will not be able to breathe from your safe second either, as it is fed from the same air supply as your main regulator. However, if both buddies are equipped with safe seconds, are well trained and observe good buddy diving practices, they offer a good measure of safety.

Self-sufficient systems include their own air source. This means that the user can immediately switch to a completely independent air supply if the main one fails without having to involve another diver. Some are nothing more than a very small tank with a built-in regulator; these are small enough to clip to a BCD and light enough for air travel. Because they contain little air, they should only be used on dives where the safety of the surface can be reached quickly and easily. Pony bottles are normal scuba tanks to which an ordinary regulator is attached. They usually contain two or three litres (0.5–0.8 gallons) of gas – about 20 to 25 per cent of a full-sized cylinder. Adventurous diving activities call for the use of full-sized cylinders, with air used progressively from each to ensure that enough air remains in each to handle an emergency gas loss at any point in the dive – even if the diver must swim some distance out of a wreck or cave or complete lengthy decompression stops. Gas-management skills are taught from entry level to help divers to avoid running out of air, with advanced procedures being used as the diving becomes more demanding. Divers are also taught how to attach, mark and deploy alternative air sources for maximum effectiveness in an emergency.

RIGHT: Emergency air supply

PRESSURE GAUGES

Pressure gauges link to the regulator first stage and indicate how much air is left in the tank. The simplest gauges are like petrol gauges: they only tell you the remaining tank pressure and you have to calculate for yourself how long the air will last. This depends on the size of your tank, your depth, your work rate, how warm you are, how relaxed you are and whether your buddy is breathing from your tank as well, because of an emergency. These gauges are connected by a hose and may be part of an instrument console.

Some dive computers incorporate a pressure gauge. They may also be connected by a hose or use a radio link from the first stage that dispenses with the hose altogether. By averaging the drop in tank pressure over a few breaths they can estimate the remaining air time. If any of the above factors alter, the computer re-estimates. By providing divers with a time based in hours and minutes they can plan more accurately, especially if making a decompression dive, as the remaining air time can be compared to the required stop time. Some computers use breathing rate as one of their decompression calculations; others know when you have switched tanks under water, as is common in technical diving. Although some computers include audible low-air alarms, you should check your air supply regularly as alarms are not always easy to hear. It is a good safeguard to check your gauge for accuracy regularly, too – it can go wrong.

CYLINDERS

Diving cylinders are simply containers for breathing gases, usually air or an oxygen-rich version of air called nitrox. Technical divers may also use other gas mixtures for breathing, such as trimix or pure oxygen, or argon for inflating dry suits for warmth.

Cylinders or tanks come in a range of capacities. Because different terms are used to discuss cylinder capacity, it is important to understand them. In the USA it is common to refer to a cylinder's full carrying load – for example, a 72 or an 80. This is the amount of air, in cubic feet, that the tank holds when filled correctly. In the UK, it is normal to talk about an empty cylinder's capacity or volume in litres – for example, 10s or 12s. Some

ABOVE: Preparing for a dive with a pair of independent cylinders

stainless steel and titanium for manufacturing diving cylinders, only steel or aluminium tanks are commonly available. Steel is generally tougher and, if compared to an aluminium cylinder of the same capacity, usually smaller and lighter in air while heavier under water. However, it corrodes more readily if moisture enters it. Aluminium is not so tough and must be thicker-walled than a steel tank to hold the same pressure. This tends to make alloy cylinders bulkier and heavier in air while lighter in the water. Counting in its favour is its resistance to corrosion.

Cylinders vary in size. Some are long and thin, other short and wide. Depending on the height of the diver, each may have its advantages. Knowledgeable divers use their cylinder as part of their trim control by adjusting its position on the back pack.

Tanks must be specially prepared for use with gases other than normal air. Check with your cylinder supplier for details. Cylinders need to be periodically inspected for signs of corrosion and metal fatigue. Laws vary in each country, and only a test house approved by the local government agency should be used.

people prefer to talk about the capacity of a tank in litres when full – perhaps 2,000 to 3,000 litres.

The amount of gas that a tank can hold is a combination of its empty volume and the pressure of the gas inside: multiply one by the other to get the true gas content. Cylinders for diving typically operate at maximum pressures of between 180 and 300 bars or 2600 to 4400 PSI. The maximum pressure that the cylinder is rated for use with is referred to as working pressure and will be stamped on the tank. Cylinders are often combined to increase the duration of a dive, for safety (see alternative air sources) or for carrying different gas mixtures by technical divers.

Scuba cylinders must be manufactured according to the specifications of government agencies. Cylinders intended for use in different countries will have different specifications and may be difficult to have filled, tested or re-certified abroad. Although attempts have been made to use carbon fibre,

ABOVE: Twin cylinders linked by a manifold

CYLINDER VALVES

All diving cylinders are equipped with valves. At their simplest, they are merely taps that turn the air on and off. Some valves accept two regulators, which has safety benefits (*see Alternative air sources*, p. 38). Regulators may be attached to the cylinder valve by a stirrup, which is universally known as an A-clamp and is popular in the UK, North America, the Red Sea region, the Caribbean and Australia. The A-clamp is not normally used with cylinders containing more than 232 bars. Another way in which to attach a regulator is to use a DIN valve. The regulator screws into the tank valve and is held in place by five or more threads. This connection is very difficult to dislodge through impact, making it popular with wreck and cave divers. DIN connectors are always used with very high-pressure cylinders, such as 300-bar models. DIN valves are popular in Scandinavia and Germany and are becoming increasingly common in the UK. To allow the use of otherwise incompatible tank valves and regulators, adapters are offered for both. However, only pressure-compatible connections should be used in order to avoid potential injury.

Special tank valves called manifolds are used to connect two or more cylinders. Some simply clamp two ordinary tank valves together, making it easy to split up the cylinders for use as singles. Others replace the single cylinder valves completely. Many manifolds allow two regulators to be used, with an on/off tap for each. If a regulator freeflows, it can be turned off and the remaining air in both tanks can be inhaled through the back-up regulator. Because a freeflowing regulator can empty both cylinders very quickly, some manifolds have an isolation valve. This lets the diver breathe from each tank separately, or from both together, by opening or closing a handwheel, minimising the risk of a catastrophic air failure. The proper use of isolation valves and gas-management skills are taught in specialist diving classes.

Some cylinders use reserve valves, which make it difficult to breathe when the cylinder pressure is low. This warns divers that they are running out of gas. By opening the reserve valve they can breathe normally again. Pressure gauges are more popular because divers can always see how much gas they have left; a reserve only indicates that they are low on air. Reserves may not provide sufficient gas for deep, decompression or under-ice dives, in caves or within wrecks where a diver cannot ascend immediately. Reserves can be tripped by accident, so that when a diver finds it hard to breathe, it is because he or she has actually run out of air completely.

Cylinder valves should always be fitted by a professional to ensure that they are compatible with the tank, regulators and breathing gases that will be used.

BUOYANCY-CONTROL DEVICES

Successful divers know that they are most comfortable and relaxed and use the least air and expend the least energy when they are in total control of their buoyancy. Controlled divers see more on each dive because they are not distracted by having to fight to stay in the exact position that they want and can glide like a fish rather than thrashing the water like a swimmer, which disturbs and frightens under water life. A diver who is skilled in buoyancy control stays off the bottom and so does not kick up clouds of silt, thereby destroying visibility or breaking coral.

ABOVE: BCDs keep you afloat on the surface

Divers' buoyancies change during a dive. As they descend, their exposure suit may compress, so that they lose buoyancy and become heavier. As they breathe, air lost from their tanks will make them lighter. A buoyancy-control device helps to overcome these differences, enabling the diver to remain neutrally buoyant and hang suspended in the water column without effort, become negative to kneel on the sand to shoot a video, or positive to ascend without finning.

The BCD is also an important safety aid at the surface, where it can be inflated to help a tired diver stay comfortably afloat without effort. If an emergency occurs under water, the BCD can be used to raise a diver who is in difficulties.

BCDs are sold in four main styles. Normally all are equipped with a direct feed or power inflator that lets divers add air from their scuba tanks to the inflatable bladder to increase buoyancy. Some also have small, refillable air tanks or one-use carbon-dioxide cylinders for back-up inflation in case the diver runs out of air. Finally, they can be inflated by mouth. To decrease buoyancy, air is vented through dump valves. Pressure-relief valves prevent too much air from bursting the bladder.

Horse-collar BCDs fit over the head like a yachting or airline life jacket. They are no longer popular because they tend to pull a diver's head up under the water – this is an unstreamlined position. A separate back pack has to be used for your tank.

Waistcoat BCDs slip on like a jacket and incorporate the tank harness. They have air chambers that run alongside the tank and help to keep the diver horizontal when under water.

Breakaway BCDs also slip on like a jacket. They are similar to waistcoat jackets, but have quick-release, adjustable shoulder straps. Some divers find these easier to put on and remove.

Back-mounted BCDs or 'wings' place all of the air alongside the tanks. They also incorporate the tank harness. Many wings are designed for technical divers who will be carrying two or more cylinders, along with heavy battery packs to power lights and salvage tools.

BCDs should be chosen according to the use to which they will be put. It is essential that the BCD has enough buoyancy or lift to support a diver properly, not only under water, but also with the diver's head held above water on the surface.

Divers using single cylinders in tropical waters with a dive skin need far less buoyancy than a trimix diver carrying five cylinders and wearing a thick, neoprene dry suit. Advice should be taken on how much buoyancy is appropriate for your style of diving. There's a wide span to choose from, ranging from 8-45kg (17.6-99.2lb), to suit different needs.

Proper sizing is also critical with most BCDs in order to ensure proper flotation or to stop the cylinder from sliding around. BCDs specifically tailored to fit women and younger divers are available.

Some BCDs are modular. By changing the harness or bladder they can accommodate a range of sizes and adapt to different diving conditions and purposes.

ABOVE: BCDs help you control your buoyancy underwater

ABOVE: BCDs make diving safe and comfortable

It is vital to weight yourself properly. Using the minimum weight that will allow you to make a controlled, shallow-water safety stop at the end of your dive with a near-empty tank should be your goal. Proper breath control and the BCD are tools that consummate divers use to fine-tune their buoyancy. They begin with proper weighting and do not use the BCD as a crutch for inadequate diving skills.

Divers who understand buoyancy control also trim themselves properly. Trim is the attitude at which a diver floats under water or at the surface. A diver usually prefers to be horizontal under the water and vertical, or inclined slightly backwards, on the surface. This keeps divers ultra-streamlined under water, while supporting them with their heads above water with good all-round visibility on the surface. Proper trim is achieved by the careful positioning of the scuba tank and weights to create the perfect balance.

BCDs are not life jackets, so achieving the correct trim can be vital on the surface where an incorrect trim can place a diver face down in the water. BCDs may include such features as spine pads to make carrying cylinders more comfortable and pockets and clips or mounting rings for carrying accessories. BCDs may also have built-in weight systems. These may be designed to replace a weight belt and will have quick-release mechanisms or may be designed to counterbalance the BCD at the surface to help the wearer stay upright.

DEPTH GAUGES

The cheapest depth gauges use a simple tube which is open at one end and rely on Boyle's law to measure depth. The deeper you dive the more difficult they become to read. These capillary gauges are subject to inaccuracies through temperature changes, though they are very accurate for shallow decompression stops and offer advantages for high-altitude diving.

Mechanical gauges, such as bourdon tube and diaphragm models, are generally accurate over normal recreational depths. Accuracy is expressed as a percentage that improves as depth decreases. They are often temperature-compensated and may be user-adjustable for high-altitude diving. Most gauges have a maximum-depth indicator in the form of a slave needle that is driven by the current depth indicator. It shows the deepest point of the dive and must be reset before the next dive.

Depth gauges are available that give measurements in metres or feet. It helps to use a depth gauge which has increments that you are familiar with. If you are diving with people who are unfamiliar with your measurements confusion can easily arise. Increments that match your dive table's increments are also helpful. Luminous markings are worthwhile.

Electronic depth gauges are the most accurate. They may incorporate electronic dive timers and ascent-rate alarms, and can log your dives.

Depth gauges should be handled with great care and should be regularly cross-checked for accuracy. They are precision instruments and even a minor inaccuracy could lead to a serious injury or worse.

ABOVE: Depth gauge

COMPASSES

Navigation is often an important part of diving pleasure and safety. Compasses help divers to find their way to and from dive sites and to relocate the boat or shore exit point while remaining under water. They are also used for searches by rescue and salvage divers.

Mechanical compasses have either a needle or card that shows the diver's course and a lubber line to assist in staying on track. Some compasses have a comparison bezel that can be used to 'memorise' the return route or another useful heading.

RIGHT: Learn to trust your compass. Electronic compasses may be able to store many different headings for recall during the dive and also have a timer for timing swims. This can make complex navigation runs easier for advanced divers.

CONSOLES

Consoles provide a way in which to group instruments together rather than attaching them to your wrists or harness. As a minimum they usually include a pressure gauge and a depth gauge or computer. A compass is often added and occasionally a knife as well. Some divers like to keep all the gauges on one side, allowing them to have quick reference to such information as air, depth and direction. Others find this kind of console too long and place one gauge on the back to reduce its length.

To avoid causing damage to both coral and your console, it should be secured closely to your body and should never be allowed to drag.

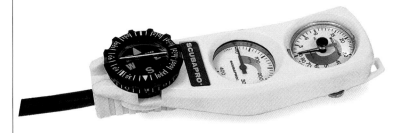

ABOVE: A console keeps all the controls comfortably to hand

WATCHES

To avoid decompression sickness and to keep to agreed time limits, divers need a timing device. Dive watches for recreational diving are normally rated to 200m (660ft) or greater. The watch industry uses different test methods to establish depth limits for timepieces to those used by diving-equipment and underwater photographic equipment suppliers. Thus a watch for actual use to 50m (164ft) should be rated to 200m (660ft).

Analogue diving watches have luminous faces or batons for easier reading at night, at depth or in low visibility. A one-way

Above: Keeping a track of time is essential

rotating bezel indicates the length of the dive. If the bezel is accidentally knocked it will indicate a longer dive time than in reality instead of a shorter one that could endanger the diver through missed decompression.

Some analogue dive watches also include digital displays, which divers can use separately to count down safety or decompression stops or to time surface intervals.

With an analogue watch, it is a good idea to check the second hand regularly during the dive to ensure that the watch has not stopped.

Digital watches usually have a back light for dark conditions. Some divers simply set the stopwatch function running to time dives and pre-set the duration of the safety stop on the countdown alarm. To avoid an accidentally pressed button halting the stopwatch, digital-watch users may shift functions, recalling the stopwatch display only when needed.

Divers' watches may also incorporate depth gauges, safety alarms and log-book functions which may be downloadable.

COMPUTERS

Diving computers are used to calculate a diver's decompression status. Some models also monitor the diver's breathing gas. Like dive tables, they are based on theory and do not actually monitor the gas in an individual's body. Computers track what

LEFT: Technology has increased the time we can spend underwater

the diver does and compare this to an algorithm (this is where the computer's decompression table or model is stored). By matching the almost infinite combinations of depths, dive times, surface intervals and repetitive dives to the computer model, the machine can then calculate how long the diver can remain under water without decompressing, the length and depth of any decompression stops, time any surface intervals, calculate decompression limits for subsequent dives, work out when it is safe to fly or ascend to altitude and also when the diver's gas levels will have returned to normal or desaturated. This information is then displayed on the machine as numbers or graphics or a combination of the two.

These calculations are quick and easy for computers to do. Dive tables, on the other hand, require the diver to do the maths and get it right every time. Moreover, tables cannot use all the figures available to the computer (there isn't enough space) and their convenience is often based on procedures that penalise the diver (by providing less time under water, for instance).

Some computers offer full decompression information, meaning that they keep divers fully informed as to the depth of the stops that they must make, and the combined time of all the stops, so that they know how long it will take to reach the surface. Others only tell divers the depth at which they must decompress and when it is safe to surface. Many computers have on-board simulators to enable divers to forecast how a future dive might be planned. A computer can often be linked to a PC to enable dive profiles to be logged directly from the dive computer's memory. Audible alarms for safety violations are now common.

Gas-integrated computers measure the gas in the diver's tank and can predict how long it will last, even if the diver's breathing rate alters. This is done using either a hose or a radio transmitter attached to the regulator. Recreational divers usually choose either air- or nitrox-compatible computers. Nitrox

machines can be set for different mixes and care must be taken to ensure that no errors are made. Nitrox computers also track oxygen levels to help avoid oxygen seizures.

Technical divers may use computers that know when they have changed gases in order to ensure the avoidance of oxygen poisoning and that proper decompression is carried out.

Just as there is a choice of dive tables, so too is there a choice of computer algorithms. Some 'smart computers' adjust themselves to take into account such factors as cold and the diver's work rate, as well as provocative dive profiles, and then increase safety margins automatically.

Dive computers need to be used with care, just like tables. Its a sensible idea to read the instruction manual for your computer before you dive with it. Many have customised functions that must be pre-set before use.

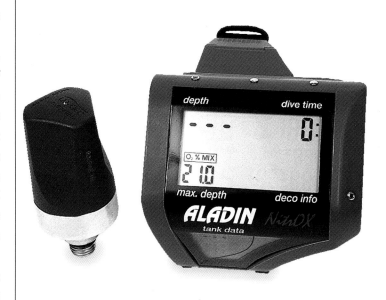

ABOVE: Some computers incorporate information direct from your scuba cylinder

BELOW AND LEFT: Computers displaying vital information

EXPOSURE SUITS

Exposure suits protect divers from becoming chilled and from abrasions and stings. Diving takes place from Antarctica to the Tropics, and the wide temperature range encountered, combined with people's individual tolerance to cold, the duration, number and depths of their dives and their activity level, means that no single exposure suit meets all needs.

In tropical waters, many recreational divers need nothing more than a bathing suit. However, a full-length body suit made of Lycra or a similar material offers some protection from jelly-fish stings and is therefore a wise precaution.

Even in the tropics divers may feel cold. Some jump suits have a layer that retains heat which may be all the extra protection that they need. These suits are known as dive skins. They are lightweight and fold up small, making them ideal for travelling.

Neoprene rubber is the most popular material for wet suits. Neoprene is full of nitrogen bubbles, which are poor heat conductors. Because the gas compresses with increasing depth, insulation and buoyancy levels reduce as a diver descends. The neoprene is normally lined with nylon or Lycra on the inside to make it easy to slip on and off. The outside may be lined with sheet or stippled rubber, which reduces heat loss from wind chill between dives, or with nylon or Lycra, which is not so resistant to wind chill when wet but increases durability and allows for a choice of colours.

To help the diver remain warm, wet suits must fit closely to prevent cold water from flowing through the suit and chilling the diver. The idea is that only a little water is allowed to enter the suit and it should remain there throughout the dive. The diver will lose some body warmth to this water as heat moves towards cold, but it will be minimal.

LEFT: Numb fingers are no fun – dress appropriately!

ABOVE: A hood keeps your head warm

Wet suits come in a variety of styles suitable for use across the broadest temperature ranges. Thin (2-3mm or 0.125in) vests and 'shorties' may be used in very warm water. Increasingly thicker, full-body suits are used as temperatures decrease. Wet suits can be bought as jump suits, jackets and trousers or long johns, or farmer johns in thick-nesses of up to 8 mm (0.275in) or more. Because neoprene becomes less supple as it becomes thicker, divers must balance comfort and ease of movement against warmth. By layering the torso with vests, the high heat-loss areas of the armpits, chest, abdomen and spine can be better protected, while leaving the legs and arms relatively unrestricted.

Heat loss from the extremities must also be avoided. A hood protects the head, from which up to 50 per cent of the body heat can be lost, and neck. Gloves or mitts and socks or boots protect the hands and feet.

For divers working in very cold water, or making prolonged dives, special features are used to minimise heat loss even further. Since there is a practical limit as to how thick the suit can be, these efforts concentrate on minimising the exchange of water through the suit. This is called flushing. Firstly the suit is tailored to sculpt the body. This avoids hollows forming in areas like the spine and armpits, where large volumes of water can collect; as the diver moves, water will be pumped in and out of these pockets, and as cold water comes into contact with the diver it will draw heat away from him or her. For most divers, modern, off-the-shelf wet suits made from supple, body-hugging neoprene will fit well enough. For those of a more challenging shape, a tailored suit may be essential. Adding seals to the wrists, face and ankles also helps to reduce water exchange. Suits with this feature are called semi-dry. Dispensing with zips also helps.

Skin divers face particular challenges when working in cooler waters. A thick wet suit requires a lot of lead. Because it has no way of compensating for lost buoyancy through the compression of the neoprene, they can become very heavy on deeper dives and divers expend great energy returning to the surface. Divers also often spend many hours in the water compared to scuba divers. To avoid using thick wet suits and still stay warm for long periods, they use wet suits that are unlined. The surface of unlined neoprene is spongy and clings to bare skin. Flushing is eliminated at the expense of durability, and the inconvenience of having to use a lubricant like talc to get the suit on.

Dry suits are an increasingly popular choice for temperate- and cold-water diving. They use special seals to prevent water entering through the neck and also have either seals at the wrists or ankles or built-in gloves or boots.

Neoprene dry suits rely mostly on the air trapped within the suit and the neoprene's poor heat conductivity to prevent heat loss. Their buoyancy and insulation decreases with depth just like wet suits. Often considerable weight is needed to offset their inherent buoyancy.

Membrane dry suits are shell suits that keep the diver dry but have no integral warmth. Divers therefore wear underclothing made of pile or Thinsulate™ that traps air to stay warm. By varying their underclothing, divers can adapt the suit to take account of many different combinations, such as depth, duration, water temperature and work load, to achieve personal comfort. These suits require much less lead than neoprene dry suits.

Because dry suits contain air which will compress with depth and cause the suit to hug the diver uncomfortably (known as 'squeezing'), an airline from the diver's main air supply lets the diver inject air as needed to counter this. Occasionally, argon is used instead of air, as this keeps the diver warmer for longer due to its poorer conductivity, though some divers have concerns about its safety. Dump valves are fitted to expel the expanding air during ascent and avoid a dangerously fast ascent. Some must be vented manually, others are automatic. Most dry-suit divers use their suits for routine buoyancy control but wear a BCD for emergency floatation and for proper support at the surface.

No one should attempt to use a dry suit without having had the proper training.

WEIGHT SYSTEMS

Most divers begin their dive positively buoyant or will become so as their tank empties during the dive. To compensate for this a weight system is used.

The most basic weight system is simply a belt onto which lead weights can be threaded and which is worn around the waist. Some belts automatically adjust for suit compression so that they do not become loose at depth or restrict breathing during the ascent. Other belts use lead shot stored in pouches. These can be more comfortable because they hug the body and avoid the hard edges of block weight systems. Some BCDs incorporate weight pockets into which block weights or packets of lead shot can be placed.

Weight harnesses are designed to allow weights to be moved around during the dive. This allows skilled divers to alter their attitudes or trim in the water for comfort or to achieve certain tasks. Ankle weights are used to help with trim control, to keep a diver horizontal in the water and to overcome problems with overly buoyant legs which some divers experience.

All weight systems should have a quick-release mechanism that makes it quick and easy to jettison the weights in an emergency.

Lead ballast can be bought in blocks of 1 to 6kg (2.2–13.2lb) or as shot. Small weights make it easier to adjust for precision buoyancy or perfect trim. Coatings, usually plastic, are more environmentally friendly, photogenic and less likely to stain your suit. Dive centres and boats will have lead weights available for hire.

ABOVE: Whichever weight system you choose, make sure you can jettison it in an emergency

TORCHES

Divers carry torches for many reasons. Even in brightly lit water a torch is still useful for restoring colours and looking into holes and under ledges. In dark conditions, at night and inside wrecks and caves, they become essential safety aids.

Torches range from tiny, one-battery, back-up lights used to read instruments to huge, 500-watt lamps powered by cylinder size. Rechargeable battery packs are used for cave exploration and filming. Most serious recreational divers have a large lantern for night diving and a smaller torch used casually during the day.

The small light is used as a back-up for night dives in case the main one fails.

Divers who are planning to enter wrecks or caves will often use three lights each. Each will have enough battery life to last for the entire dive. Because lights can flood, batteries fail and bulbs blow, and a light failure in these conditions can be fatal, two back-ups are usually considered the minimum.

Rechargeable lights can be an attractive option for regular users. They are less costly to run than torches that use disposable batteries. Not all chargers will work world-wide because of differences in voltages. Some dive centres and boats do not run their generators long enough to provide a full charge.

Dive lights can be either secured with wrist lanyards or mounted to other equipment using clips.

STROBES

Strobes are flashing lights used by divers to indicate their position to others. Many divers only switch them on if a problem develops. They are normally clipped high on the diver's body so that they are easily visible to people on the shore or in the boat. Strobes may also be used to mark anchor and shot lines or dive sites to aid location at night or in poor visibility.

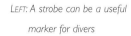

LEFT: A strobe can be a useful marker for divers

LEFT AND ABOVE: Big or small, a torch is a handy tool for the diver

BELOW: Exploring a Red Sea wreck by lamplight

KNIVES

Diving knives are not weapons of aggression or defence, but tools. Divers are not the only people with an interest in lakes, rivers and oceans. Fishermen, too, use these waters. The same thing – fish – often attracts both. Many dive sites carry a very real risk of entanglement in lost lines or nets. The diving knife's primary purpose is to enable divers to cut themselves or their buddies free if an entanglement occurs. Knives come in a range of lengths and designs. Most have a sharp, plain edge for slashing weeds like kelp or thin, monofilament lines and a serrated edge for sawing through heavier lines or ropes. Some also have a notch called a line-cutter that makes it easier to trap and cut lines. Knife blades represent a compromise. Pure steel rusts quickly in sea water, so alloys are added to inhibit this. The more alloy that is used, the more difficult it is to hone the blade and keep an edge. The benefit is less corrosion and reduced maintenance. Diving-knives are made to sink; if you are

ABOVE: Not a toy! Diving knives are mostly used to cut entangling nets

trapped and you lose your grip, you don't want your knife to float to the surface.

A sheath is used for carrying the knife and should have a secure, but easily operated release. Divers normally place their knives where they can be reached with either hand. The calf, thigh and BCD harness are popular mounting points for knives. Many divers carry two knives, one being used as a hammering and prying general-purpose tool, the other being a small, sharp knife for emergency use only. These are often placed on a BCD hose or else on the bicep or forearm. Some divers also use a curly cord similar to a telephone cable to secure their knives to their sheaths. However, some divers have been injured by knives recoiling on these cables.

Because monofilament mesh nets can be hard to cut with ordinary knives, some divers also carry net scissors.

LEFT: Small is beautiful! A pair of net scissors can cut just as well as a knife

MARKER BUOYS

Marker buoys may be towed by a diver throughout the dive to make it easier for a boat to follow them. A dive flag attached to the float warns other craft that there are divers below and therefore to stay clear. Buoys can be used to carry extra equipment like cameras, soft drinks for refreshment when skin diving and also to mark dive sites.

REELS

Reels are used by divers to tow marker buoys, deploy rescue tubes from depth, carry out searches and for penetration dives into wrecks, caves or beneath the ice.

RESCUE TUBES / DELAYED-MARKER BUOYS

Many divers carry inflatable rescue tubes. There are many versions, but they are all used to make the diver more obvious on the surface. Some are designed so that a diver can inflate them under water and use them to hang from during decompression or safety stops. These are called delayed-marker buoys to indicate their use.

RESCUE FLAGS

Like rescue tubes these make a diver easier to locate at the surface by increasing the distance from which the diver can be seen. They can be clipped alongside the scuba tank until needed.

AIR WHISTLES

Air whistles are safety aids and work like a siren to attract attention. They connect to the BCD direct feed and depend on tank pressure to work.

LIFTING BAGS

Salvage divers use lifting bags to float finds to the surface. They work like balloons and are normally filled with air from the diver's own air supply. Some divers use them instead of rescue tubes for making safety and decompression stops.

4

TOP DIVING AROUND THE WORLD

Diving introduces you to a completely new world — a world that comprises two thirds of the earth's surface. The creatures you find beneath the waves, along with the seascape, plants and general conditions, vary as widely as they do on land. Whether you prefer exploring coral reefs swarming with fish of every colour in the rainbow, weaving your way through swaying green-gold kelp forests with playful seals, investigating caves and labyrinth tunnels, or searching for sunken treasure on ancient wrecks, you are sure to have a great experience once you duck your head under the water.

ABOVE: *Beautiful coral displayed in clear tropical waters*

THE RED SEA

The Red Sea is surrounded by a dry, parched desert landscape, completed by a mountainous skyline. This monotone landscape belies the colourful reefs full of life that exist underwater. The Red Sea lies on the northern section of the Great Rift Valley, the fault line between the African and the Asian continents, with most of its coastline along Egypt, Saudi Arabia and Eritrea. The waters, which come from the Indian Ocean at the southernmost end of the sea, are warm and literally bursting with marine life. There are Red Sea dwarf wrasse, jewel fairy basslets, royal angelfish, damselfish, cardinals, butterflyfish and any number of wrasse, parrotfish, large groupers, red and black snapper, triggerfish, surgeonfish and unicornfish.

At the larger end of the fish spectrum, there are honeycomb moray eels, eagle and manta rays and pufferfish. Sharks too, are plentiful here and several species can be found including the Red Sea lemon shark, and hammerhead and zebra sharks if you are lucky. Turtles are often seen on dives too, and dolphins regularly chaperone the boats. The coral is healthy and there is a wide variety of hard and soft corals. Sponges and anemones nestle between.

Certain areas within the Red Sea have suffered in past years due to extensive tourism, but recently the Egyptian government has cracked down on boat and tour operators in the area. Local dive centres are strict with divers on their boats, and care for the underwater environment is taken extremely seriously. Some

ABOVE: Clownfish stay close to their anemones
BELOW: The trumpetfish will keep his eye on you!

areas have been declared off limits, and in others the dive boats must have a park ranger on board to be able to operate legally. There are various areas that have now been declared national marine parks, such as the Ras Mohammed area.

WRECK-DIVING IN THE RED SEA

The Red Sea is not only renowned for its marine life, it has some excellent wrecks to explore, and there are also the remains of Cousteau's Conshelf experiment. His idea was to create an underwater habitat. Conshelf II was, in the end, a successful submarine habitat, and a team of five men stayed in it for more than a month. One of the modules from Conshelf II in Sha'ab Rumi remains relatively intact and is still airtight.

Exploring the wrecks of the Red Sea is a must: the *Thistlegorm* is legendary – a British cargo ship which sank in 1940 during an air raid in the Strait of Gobal, between Sha'ab Ali reef and the Sinai coast. It sank with a huge cargo: supplies of Wellington boots, trucks, two locomotives, ammunition and motorcycles.

The *Carnatic* sank in 1869 when it hit a reef, only five years after it was built. It was carrying 230 passengers and a cargo of gold, most of which was salvaged, but in 1870 the *Carnatic* shifted, and no one knows where the rest of the gold is now.

The *Ghiannis D* is another interesting wreck to explore. Although there is little marine life on this Greek cargo ship, it is particularly photogenic – underwater photographers will find it extremely rewarding.

BELOW: Every anemone has its own inhabitants

For those that have no interest in wrecks there are plenty of other things to see. Ras Mohammed is a broad peninsula projecting seawards from the tip of the Sinai. The tip of the peninsula offers some of the most spectacular diving found anywhere in the world. There are caves and overhangs, fringe reefs, eel gardens and wall dives where every ledge and crevice has some interesting animal hiding in it. It does have permanent strong currents all year round though, so a good dive guide is recommended. In the summer the nutrient-rich water is at its warmest and the reef becomes a magnet to large schools of pelagic fish – barracuda, snapper, jackfish and batfish – silky, sandbar, oceanic whitetip and blacktip sharks, hammerheads and dolphins.

NB Temperature: 'summer' *refers to May to September,* **'winter'** *is October to April, unless stated otherwise.*
All measurements, *(metres, km, celsius, etc) are given in imperial equivalent.*
Decompression chamber: Yes *means that there is a decompression chamber within 50km of the dive sites mentioned. Often there are sites mentioned that are very far apart – the decompression chamber may not be within 50km of all of these sites.*

USEFUL INFORMATION

Climate: Dry and sunny. From May to September the temperature ranges between 38 and 41°C (100–105°F), and from October through to April the temperature is between 23 and 29°C (71–84°F). The water temperature ranges between 25 and 27°C (78–80°F) in the warmer months, and 19 and 21°C (66–70°F) otherwise.

Currents: Usually quite easy to predict as the Red Sea has only one very narrow outlet at its extreme southern end. The tidal currents aren't dangerously strong, but it is always best to check first with someone who knows the area well. There are, of course, localised currents which you should also be aware of.

Visibility: Can vary according to the temperature of the water. Sometimes plankton blooms occur when cooler water is warmed, but generally visibility is good to excellent.

Decompression chamber: Yes.

MALDIVES

ooking like grains of sand scattered in a never-ending sea, the Maldives are located about 650km (400miles) south-east of India, and the atolls extend 760km (475miles) north to south. There are more than 1,000 islands, subdivided among nineteen atolls, of which only 200 are inhabited. The island of Male, which lies in the centre of the archipegalo, has the only real city in the Maldives. Lush vegetation grows on the islands, with many lakes and streams providing water for the plantlife.

The Maldives are formed by the summit of an underwater mountain chain rising from depths of 4,000m (11,330ft) up to shallows of 70m (200ft). None of the 298 square km (73,640 acres) of visible land is more than three metres above sea level, so all the houses are built on stilts.

The underwater world is unsurpassable — reefs that seem to go on forever, seascapes of mountains, valleys, chasms and cliffs, with a marine life so rich and diverse it is hard to know where to begin describing it. Due to its position in the middle of the Indian Ocean, with 2km (1.25 miles) drops into the depths around the atolls, migratory currents flow through and leave abundant plankton behind for marine life to feed on. Reef fish are plentiful and diverse, but hammerheads, whale sharks, tunas and orcas are also visitors. The corals are magnificent, with soft corals of almost every colour imaginable, providing an appropriate setting for the shoals of silver trevallys, red coral groupers, giant cod and a huge variety of other species.

ABOVE: *Spectacular lionfish*
BELOW: *Custom-built dive-boat*

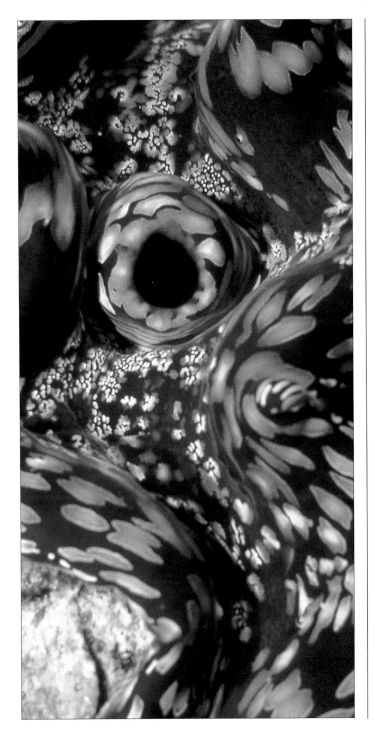

ABOVE: Nudibranchs make great photographic subjects – they move slowly!

LEFT: The multi-coloured mantle of the sea-clam

Ari atoll, situated fairly centrally in this huge archipegalo, is probably most famous for its manta rays. It is an ideal spot for plankton-feeders which is why so many manta rays thrive here. There is a strong current which brings the micro-organisms on which the manta rays feed.

There are also several wrecks to explore. The *Maldive Victory* sank in 1981 and is now lying at a depth of 35m (99ft) in the North-Male atoll. As it is such a recent wreck it is still fairly intact, although various marine animals have already adopted it as their home. There are two wrecks on the Lhaviyani atoll, easy to spot because one of them rises five metres (14ft) out of the water! Both the wrecks were refrigerator ships, Japanese-registered, and no plausible reason has been given to explain why they sank in 1980. However, the wrecks are entirely encrusted with coral and there are many fish which reside in and around them. Shoals of resident glassfish part like curtains as you swim around the wreck, and batfish are regular companions on most dives here.

USEFUL INFORMATION

Water temperature: Usually 28°C (82°F) in the summer, and 27°C (80°F) in the winter.

Climate: Average temperature in the summer is between 30 and 31°C (86–88°F), in the winter it ranges from 29 to 30°C (84–86°F).

Currents: Vary dramatically from site to site. However, due to the depths surrounding the atolls, they can be quite forceful. But there are always dive sites where they are more gentle.

Visibility: Good to excellent.

Decompression chamber: Yes.

SOUTH AFRICA

South Africa has a turbulent political history, but this should not dissuade keen divers from exploring the wide variety of underwater worlds that can be found here. There is coldwater diving to be had around the Cape Town area, where Antarctic currents provide suitable conditions for animals such as Cape fur seals. There are also coral reefs, and caves and wrecks to explore along the western coastline.

The waters off Dyer Island are home to the legendary great white shark, which is often portrayed as a vicious man-eater. The resulting reputation it has is largely undeserved and they are magnificent creatures to observe. The best way to see them is to join the South African White Shark Research Institute who allow members to help on research dives.

On the eastern coast, the influence of the Indian Ocean becomes marked and you can see many of the tropical species you would expect to see in the Red Sea or the Maldives. The reefs are healthy and colourful, and if you are lucky you may spot the raggy-toothed shark, a sleek predator with teeth to fit its name.

USEFUL INFORMATION

Water temperature: In the south it is chilly all year-round – polar upwellings maintain temperatures between 9 and 14°C (48–58°F). Things warm up as you move north, with Natal sites offering positively tropical temperatures of 20°C (68°F) and above.

Climate: Dry and sunny for most of the year. Average yearly rainfall is less than 50cm (18in) for most of the country. From November to April temperatures are in the mid- to upper twenties (78–84°F) for most of the country, with temperature lows rarely below 10°C (50°F) in the south, 30°C (86°F) on the north coast. South Africa's mid-summer is in December, its mid-winter in June.

Currents: Moderate to strong.
Visibility can range from just a few metres (several feet) on a stormy day in the south, to well over 20m (57ft) in the north.

Decompression chamber: Yes.

KENYA

Kenya conjures up images of wild animal safaris, with a hot burning sun on savanna landscapes and has only recently been recognized for what it has to offer underwater, rather than on land. Few people realise what wonderful things can be seen beneath the sea. There are a myriad little islands close to the mainland, but it is the island of Pemba, 145km (90miles) off the Kenyan coast, that gives this stretch of water its name. It actually belongs to Tanzania, but Kenyan dive operators will take you there or you can dive the Kenyan side of the channel, which has plenty to see. The Pemba Channel has a reef running alongside it, as long as the whole Kenyan coast, making it one of the longest in the world. The Channel itself has depths of up to one km (0.6214 miles), making it a popular route for migrating whales, including pilot whales, humpback whales and a number of pelagic fish.

There is plenty to see underwater: lionfish, moorish idols, pufferfish, parrotfish, and a number of species of rays. Enormous gorganian fans waft on the healthy reefs, and there are numerous hard and soft corals too – as many as 30-40 different coral species can be seen on every dive. Giant groupers, giant clams, butterflyfish, angelfish, sweetlips, snappers, turtles, and batfish are just some of the fish you can expect to see. If you are a careful observer you will also come across anemone shrimps, crocodilefish, and even leaffish.

USEFUL INFORMATION

Climate: Dry and very hot. The average temperature from May to September is 29°C (84°F), and from October through to April it is even hotter, at 31°C (88°F).

Currents: Strong currents in deeper waters, but calmer waters can be found.

Visibility: Fair to good.

Decompression chamber: Yes.

ABOVE: A diver examines soft corals in warm blue waters

THAILAND

Thailand is a popular tourist destination in its own right, but in the last ten years or so the Andaman coast, with its combination of beautiful beaches, framed by dramatic limestone cliffs, healthy coral reefs, and teeming fish life has been attracting more and more divers. There seems to be something for everyone here, with great soft corals, a rich variety of fish life, varied invertebrate life, pelagics such as manta rays and whale sharks, and a dramatic underwater topography.

The Similan Islands National Marine Park, off the west coast of Thailand, includes nine granite islands and only two of them are inhabited. On the eastern side of the islands you can enjoy gentle currents and generally easy diving conditions, with white sandy sea-beds and sloping, predominantly hard coral reefs. However, if you want more dramatic scenery, try the west-facing sites with heaps of huge granite boulders, archways, tunnels and swimthroughs. There are plenty of filter feeders, nudibranchs and other molluscs, colourful sponges and tunicates, as well as crustaceans. Shoals of jacks, mackerel, and dog-tooth tuna are seen regularly. Larger marine animals such as manta rays, leopard sharks, and whale sharks can be spotted in the nearby Surin Islands.

USEFUL INFORMATION

Water temperature: Ranges from 26 to 29°C (78–84°F).

Climate: Tropical, with a dry and rainy season. The dry season is from November through to April, giving sunny skies, balmy breezes and occasional brief evening showers. This is high season when most visitors go to Thailand. Wet weather is common from May to October, but the sun shines on most days. This season has the advantage of thinner crowds and prices are cheaper. The temperature is usually between 31 and 33°C (88–92°F), staying this temperature through the rainy season and rising a few degrees in the dry season.

Currents: Can be strong on certain sites that are far out at sea, but are mild around shallow reef dives.

Visibility: Generally good. Better in the dry season.

Decompression chamber: Yes.

MALAYSIA

This is where you can see turtles resting beneath coral ledges, sailfin gobies hiding in holes, jewel anemones and comical yellow boxfish that bob about among the coral formations, and manta rays that sweep through the scene. Malaysia has an interesting underwater world, partly because it has a number of coastlines on different landmasses. It consists of the Malaysian peninsular which shares a border with Thailand, and incorporates Sarawak and Sabah in northern Borneo. Along the Borneo coast lie countless sandbanks and palm-coated islands ringed by white sandy beaches. There are few places in the world where you can swim with turtles, manta rays, schooling tuna, jacks and pelagic sharks, dive beneath a jetty to find an astounding array of critters, and then relax at night while watching the turtles lay their eggs onshore.

Sipadan and Mabul off Borneo's north-east coast, are favourites with divers. Sipadan, a small island – only one square km (100ha or 0.3861 miles), with its compact jungle, was set aside in the 1930s as a habitat for rare birdlife, but this has been gradually cleared to accommodate more guest houses, resort workers and electricity generators. Sipadan is an idyllic tropical island with lush rainforest, beautiful reefs and incredibly friendly

USEFUL INFORMATION

Climate: Warm, sunny and humid all year. This tropical climate with abundant rain has given the country a rich variety of flora and fauna and created exquisite landscapes. Wet monsoon season from December to March, dry monsoon from May to November. Layang Layang closed to tourists from November to March because of high waves and torrential rains. Pulau Mabul and Pulau Sipadan are protected by the land mass of Borneo and can be dived and visited all year round. Temperatures range between 25 and 32°C (76–88°F).

Currents: Vary widely from area to area and with time of year; check with local dive guides. Best time to go is between April and October.

Visibility: See above.

Decompression chamber: Yes.

ABOVE: *Don't forget to look up, sometimes!*

BELOW: *Turtles seem to be everywhere in these seas*

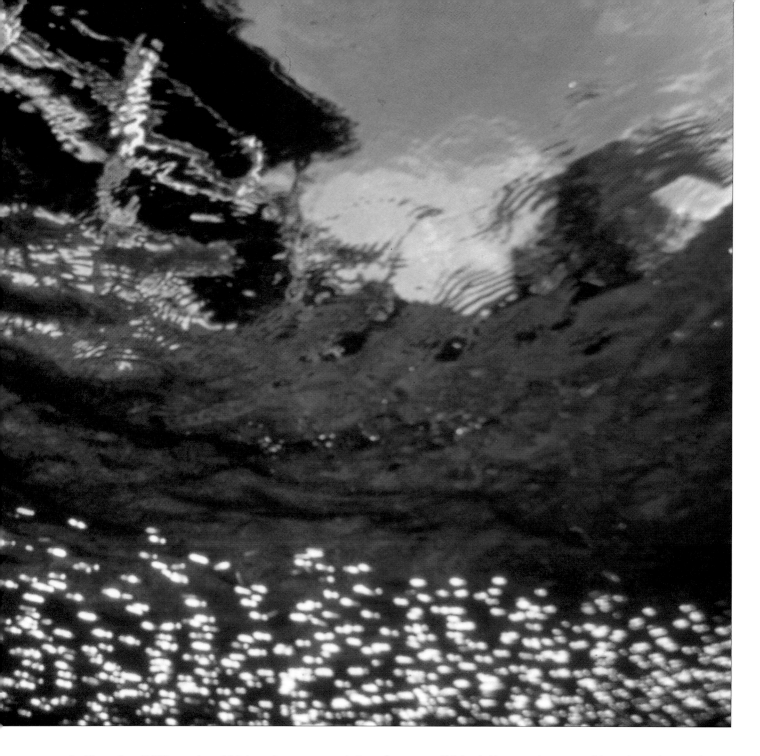

people. More than 3,000 species of fish have been seen and classified here. The island's success is partly due to its location as it is too far from the mainland for much commercial fishing to go on and the underwater fauna has been left untouched.

Mabul, at the north-eastern tip of Borneo, is a small, sandy island – a little larger than Sipadan, but it has not been so extensively developed so still offers a rustic 'untravelled' feel. Although there is still extensive fishing going on in the area, it is certainly worth a visit. Much of the local shark population has been killed – the fins are sold mainly in the Far East for sharkfin soup or for their purported medicinal properties. But it does hold a number of rare and unusual creatures that are not to be found in other parts of Malaysia. You can also see a wide variety of 'macro' creatures here – ideal for underwater photographers. There are muck dives to be had as well, when the bizarre and wonderful creatures that dwell in the murkier sand and muddy sea-bed rather than the colourful reefs can be observed.

Layang Layang at the north-western tip of Malaysian Borneo, was once a naval base and due to its isolated position enjoys untouched reefs and very few visitors. It is an area that is incredibly rich in wildlife and has amazingly diverse marine life. Here you can find virgin reefs and large specimens of pelagics. There are stunning wall dives with drop offs into the deeps, but shallow depths with beautiful coral gardens are all around too.

INDONESIA

Indonesia with its 14,000 islands, where the modern urban world coexists alongside a traditional way of life that hasn't changed for centuries, is a fascinating country to explore. The underwater world, however, is no less so, presenting a veritable cornucopia of life. Above water, Indonesia is amazing enough to almost make you forget the wonderland under the surrounding sea. There are national parks with all kinds of creatures, treks to take your breath way, and plenty of white, sandy beaches. Virtually every island is ringed by stunning coral, and you can dive a different site every day of the year without getting bored. Indonesia offers great variety in diving – the coral walls off Sulawesi, the Lembeh Strait with its weird muck-dwelling critters, the sea mounts in Maluku, beautiful coral gardens east of Ambon, and many more.

In Indonesia you are guaranteed stunning, pristine coral crowded with even more brilliantly coloured reef fish. There are schooling tuna – each one reaching up to two metres long, massive swarms of jacks and as many sharks as you choose to look at. It boasts a larger number of fish and coral species than any other spot on earth (apart from Papua New Guinea, which is very similar).

SOME OF THE DIVE SITES

Ambon, a small island nestling close to the south coast of Seram Island, west of Papua New Guinea, has good diving conditions, some excellent sites and relatively few divers.

The Bunaken/Manado Tua Marine Park is a few km offshore of Manado. It is a true natural wonder, covering more than 75,000 hectares (185,00 acres) around the islands. These reefs, are claimed by some to be the finest in the world, where coral growth continues into the depths of the sheer walls. Fish life is diverse, with good numbers of sharks, rays, tuna and jacks, and turtles too.

Flores is a relatively new diving destination and most sites have easy profiles for new or inexperienced divers, but it also provides the possibility of exploring new sites for divers with more experience. It lies further east of Java and Bali in the Indonesian island chain.

The Gili islands are a more serene version of Bali's full-on tourist infrastructure, with peaceful palm-thatched cottages on quiet beaches. The Gilis are a group of three tiny islands off Lombok's north coast, each with a subtly different flavour, but all offer resort facilities, guest houses and restaurants as well as access to dive centres. Gili Trawangan is the largest and liveliest of the islands. Gili Meno is the smallest and most tranquil. Gili Air is a mix between the two.

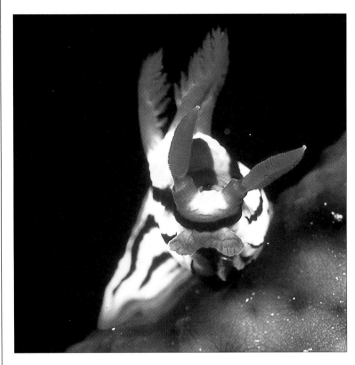

ABOVE: *Nudibranchs display an awesome range of colours*
RIGHT: *Descending to all the beauties of the coral reef*

USEFUL INFORMATION

Water temperature: Average is 26°C (79°F); lowest 23°C (74°F).

Climate: In dry season (May–September) the temperature is usually 30 or 31°C (86–88°F). In monsoon season, from October to April, the temperature drops a couple of degrees. In Maluku it shifts to April through July. Diving is better in the dry season.

Currents: Indonesia has very complex current patterns. Sites may have strong upwellings or downcurrents. Check with a local dive guide.

Visibility: Good to excellent (unless muck-diving).

Decompression chamber: Yes.

PAPUA NEW GUINEA

Papua New Guinea has more marine species than any other region in the world, and new species are being discovered all the time, as are new dive sites, which makes Papua New Guinea an exciting place to dive. It is one of the world's last remaining true wildernesses. The abundance of its wildlife, both above and below water, is astounding, with mountains, volcanoes, rivers, swamps and rainforest on land, and then coral gardens, wall reefs and marine life of spectacular colours, shapes and forms beneath the sea.

Papua New Guinea, with its fertile lands and unkempt highlands, lies roughly 720km (450miles) from the north coast of Australia. The coast of Papua New Guinea was first visited by foreigners in the late 19th century. These were missionaries and traders, although it is believed that Papua New Guineans themselves had settled there from Asia more than 50,000 years earlier. It was not until the 1930s that the first foreign explorers dared to go into the highland valleys that are the core of Papua

USEFUL INFORMATION

Water temperature: Varies between 26 and 27°C (78–80°F) in May to September, and is usually 28°C (82°F) the rest of the year.

Climate: Temperatures vary from 27 to 29°C (80–84F) from May to September, from October to April between 29 and 31°C (84–88°F). Papua New Guinea is blessed with year-round diving, but the weather can be unpredictable.

Current: Due to the very deep water close to shore, which creates upwellings of rich, plankton-rich water for the marine life to feed on, calm surfaces may disguise a moderately strong current underneath.

Visibility: Varies due to the many waterways that distribute fresh water and nutrients into the sea, causing a slight haze to develop where they intermix. This is also what provides the basics for the rich variety of marine life.

Decompression chamber: No – nearest is in Queensland, Australia.

New Guinea. The coast offers divers the opportunity to experience untouched reefs, superb marine life and a wide range of coral species.

SOME OF THE DIVE SITES

Kimbe Bay, in Walindi on the island of New Britain off the north-eastern coast of Papua New Guinea, is enclosed by mighty volcanic peaks, giving it a dramatic atmosphere. The majority of dives take place on sea mounts, or pinnacles that rise up from the sea-bed. These underwater mountains rise from depths of 300m (850ft) to just a little below the surface. The marine life that exists on these underwater mountains is extraordinary – it is a real aquatic jungle swarming with life: sea anemones in pretty pinks, deep purples, blues and greens are home to anemonefish, and butterflyfish, angelfish, parrotfish, and wrasse busy themselves among the corals. If you are vigilant you may also spot an octopus secreted in a crevice. As if this were not enough, there is also the opportunity to discover new species yourself here.

Milne Bay is the largest and least disturbed of all Papua New Guinea's coastal areas and has a veritable profusion of marine growth. Due to its position on the tip of eastern Papua New Guinea, situated between the Coral Sea and the Solomon Sea, the sea's surging movement creates plankton-rich lagoon waters for the most incredible creatures to dwell in.

Kavieng, north of New Britain, has giant schools of barracuda and eagle rays, silvertip sharks, drift dives, a maze of islands and passages, inside lagoons, mangroves and calm waters. Walindi has exquisite reefs, and encounters with whales are frequent here. There are also killer whales and dolphins. However, it is the extraordinary richness of life, combined with rare and usual creatures that can be seen that makes this place such an exciting area to dive.

FIJI

Despite the Fijian people's history of cannibalism and extreme aggression, Fiji is now noted for the friendliness and hospitality of its inhabitants. It was until fairly recently a relatively unexplored area. The island's now-vanished inhabitants, the Lapiti people, with their fearsome reputation, probably deterred a lot of would-be settlers. From the 1870s Indian labourers worked on plantations in Fiji, and 45 per cent of today's friendly Fijians are the descendants of these workers.

Above: It's not just divers who appreciate the beautiful coral in Fiji

There are 300 islands in the archipelago, with the two largest ones, Vit Levu and Vanua Levu, supporting 90 per cent of the population. The friendliness of the Fijians extends to welcoming you with an offer to share a traditional Kava drink with them. Kava is a mild narcotic and most foreigners who politely accept this find themselves, with a less than pleasant taste in their mouths and a numb tongue.

Underwater, Fiji has glorious displays of soft corals, and altogether it has more than 600 species of hard and soft corals. There are strong currents here, so much of the diving is drift diving. These currents help to provide food for the diverse fish life and pelagic species. Fan corals, such as gorgonians thrive in the plankton-rich currents, as do crinoids, and this is where you will find brightly-coloured shrimps and odd-looking squat lobsters. Turtles are often seen, and if you are lucky you may spot humpback whales cruising through.

USEFUL INFORMATION

Climate: The wet season runs from November through to April and coincides with the cyclone season. In eastern Fiji cyclones are rare and seas are extremely calm most of the time. The water temperature ranges between 25 and 28°C (77–82°F).

Currents: Can be dangerously strong, check with local dive guide.

Visibility: Best visibility is between May and October, but this is also when the water is coldest.

Decompression chamber: Yes.

AUSTRALIA

The Great Barrier Reef is Australia's, if not the world's, most famous dive site. The coral reef stretches 2,500km (1550 miles) along the Queensland coast of north-east Australia. Within the reef there are more than 600 islands, thousands of individual reefs, 1,500 species of fish, and 350 species of coral. Hard to beat! The Barrier Reef became a World Heritage listed area in the late 70s, administered by the Great Barrier Reef Marine Park Authority which instituted a strict zoning policy. This allows for the reefs to be 'rested' every few years. It also has strictly enforced rules to minimise damage resulting from tourism. Divers are 'policed' to make sure they dive according to safe guidelines and that they do not damage the aquatic environment. It is the largest marine park in the world, and it is due to the strict park policies that despite huge numbers of tourists diving there, it still has coral growth and fish life to truly astound and amaze.

Ningaloo reef, on the north-western cape of Australia is a virtually untouched barrier reef extending 260km (160miles). Its proximity to shore means you can literally walk off the beach on to a great dive site. The area has been declared a protected marine park and the state of the coral and fish life is a testament to this protection. Turtles nest up on the brilliant white sandy shore, and beyond the reef, in deep waters, humpback whales pass through on their migratory routes, and there are dolphins and dugongs in the surrounding area also. Ningaloo Reef and the Great Barrier Reef are good places to come to see coral spawning – a fantastic sight of thousands of coral sperm and eggs being released in to the water where the eggs are then fertilised. After being carried along by the currents they eventually come to a resting point where they settle and grow. However, what Ningaloo Reef is probably best known for is the whale sharks which gather off the coast – an amazing sight as their huge mouths gape open to take in as much plankton as possible.

USEFUL INFORMATION

Climate: December to March in the north and central sections is cylcone season, with September to November best.

Currents: Gentle to moderate on most sites.

Visibilty: Good to excellent.

Decompression chamber: Yes.

Above: Sunlight penetrates to the reef crest on the Barrier Reef

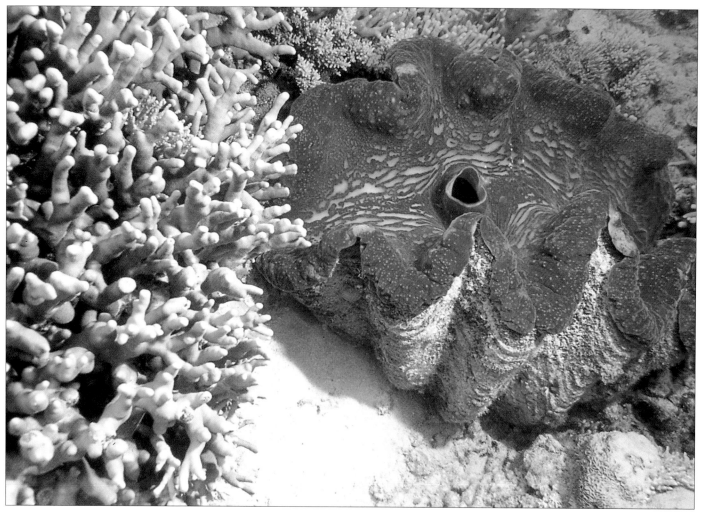

Above: The multi-coloured mantle of the clam defies description

NEW ZEALAND

New Zealand is probably not the first place most people would think of when they consider scuba diving, but it has some stunning dive sites and is equally beautiful on land. The Poor Knights Islands are, according to Jacques Cousteau, one of the world's top ten dive sites. They are the remains of an ancient string of volcanoes, now long dead. When the sea level changed during the Ice Age these volcanoes were underwater and have been shaped and carved by the sea since then, leaving caves, tunnels and archways to explore. The East Auckland current from the north coast of Australia flows across the Tasman Sea and down the continental shelf of Northland, bringing warm water and tropical marine life which settles at the Poor Knights Islands. It was declared a marine reserve in 1980, enabling the huge variety of fish, molluscs, anemones and feather stars to continue their existence unhampered. The land plunges quite suddenly down to 50m, creating great wall diving with gorgonians, lots of black coral growth, and beautiful golden kelp fronds swaying in the currents. There are sponges, barnacles, and tubeworms, seasquirts, featherstars and molluscs.

USEFUL INFORMATION

Currents: Moderate.

Climate: The air and water temperature varies dramatically throughout New Zealand – it is relatively warm in the north, and cold in the south. The water temperature around Poor Knights Island has an average of 17°C (64°F).

Visibility: Fair to good.

HAWAII

Hawaii is a tropical paradise, with swaying palms, exotic flowers, fruits, and jungle plants. Endless white sandy beaches are lapped by crystal clear waters. Within the Hawaiian archipelago, Hawaii itself is the biggest island but there are a number of other islands within the archipelago, giving you plenty of dive options. Underwater Hawaii is a maze of tunnels, archways, cathedrals, caverns and caves formed by volcanic lava over the years. It has many endemic species both above and below the sea, which is what makes it so special. There are turtles, squid, crustaceans, octopus, moray eels, dolphins and whales. For the historically oriented, there are also plenty of wrecks to be investigated – sunken tanks and jeeps, abandoned after World War II, now blanketed with corals. Many of the Hawaiian Islands have been heavily commercialised with luxury hotels available and little of the traditional lifestyle still visible. On Oahu, at the north-westerly end of the Hawaiian island chain, there is a bay formed from an ancient volcanic crater and this is a state marine reserve. There are green sea turtles of all sizes at Maunalua Bay and morays and eagle rays with their distinctive mottled back-pattern. Maui Island, just north of Hawaii, gives access to other islands such as Lanai, Molokai, Molokini and Kahoolawe and here you can see whale sharks and humpback whales, but usually only in the winter months. There are also some great cave dives. The shoreline is protected from winds, allowing delicate formations of coral to grow.

USEFUL INFORMATION

Water temperature: A few degrees below the air temperature.

Climate: Temperatures in the summer are usually around 31°C (88°F). In the winter a few degrees lower.

Currents: Moderate to strong.

Visibility: Good to excellent.

Decompression chamber: Yes.

ABOVE: Beautiful beach scene off Maui Island, Hawaii

FLORIDA KEYS

The Florida Keys is a string of islands, stretching over 325km (200miles) from Key Largo to the Dry Tortugas. Fringing the Keys are the only living reefs on mainland USA. Designated a National Marine Sanctuary in the late 1980s, the area is known for its mangroves and seagrass, which offer a comfortable habitat for lobsters, shrimp, tarpon and snapper. Because the Keys are easily accessible and diving is well established here, this is the most popular diving area for North Americans. Not only does the area attract divers and snorkellers, but also campers, bird watchers and fishermen.

A wide variety of marine life can be seen around the reefs. You may find yourself negotiating huge brain corals and marveling at huge purple sea fans, along with schools of snapper, goatfish and parrotfish. Most divers however, come for the dolphins and nurse sharks. One of the best ways to see the magnificent marine life in this area is to volunteer for an activity run by many of the organisations that research and monitor the marine environment in the Florida Keys. You may find yourself becoming involved in a coral survey, fish research or helping to clean up the reefs.

Wreck divers can find something of interest here also: the *City Washington* and the *Benwood* are two popular shallow dives, while the *Bibb* and *Duane* are more challenging wrecks for experienced divers. Above ground, divers may like to visit the famous statue of Christ in John Pennekamp Park. This was given to the Underwater Society of America in 1961 by a well-known industrialist at the time, Egide Cressi. Its bottom is at 6m (17ft) with the top at 3m (9ft) below the surface.

ABOVE: *Friendly divemasters unloading the boat after a tiring day's diving*

MEXICO

The land of lost civilisations also has great diving to offer. Cozumel, just off the Yucatàn peninsula, offers some excellent diving. On the west side of the island there are great shallow snorkelling reefs and also a deep barrier reef that can be dived on. There are long stretches of virgin reef to be explored and a 30km (20miles) section of Cozumel's coral reef has been designated a marine sanctuary. Here you can do some exhilarating drift diving. There are winding tunnels and canyons of coral to explore, covered with sea fans, and yellow and orange sponges. There are huge barrel sponges, and whip coral with angelfish, rays, and turtles and groupers weaving their way through.

USEFUL INFORMATION

Water temperature: Warm, 28°C (83°F) in the summer and 22°C (72°F) in the winter.

Climate: Temperature is usually a hot 31 or 32°C (89–91°F) in the summer, and 25°C (77°F) in the winter.

Current: Visibility is amazing here from 30–45m (85–130ft) all year, sometimes reaching 65–70m (185–200ft).

Decompression chamber: Yes.

USEFUL INFORMATION

Water temperature: Warm, 28°C (82°F) in the summer and dropping to 27°C (81°F) in the winter.

Climate: Temperature is usually a hot 32 or 33°C (90–92F) in the summer, and 31°C (88°F) in the winter.

Current: Visibility is amazing here from 30–45m (85–130ft) all year, sometimes reaching 65–70m (185–200ft).

Decompression chamber: Yes.

ABOVE: Barrel sponges abound off the Keys

GALAPAGOS

COCOS ISLANDS

There is never a dull moment in the waters surrounding the Galapagos Islands, with mischievous sealions, innumerable turtles, comical penguins, 'prehistoric' marine iguanas and schooling hammerhead sharks. The Galapagos Islands are world famous as the place that Charles Darwin chose to visit in order to find evidence to support the biblical version of creation. The plan didn't quite work out, and the result was his book on evolutionary theory: *The Origin of Species*. The waters are nutrient-rich due to the cold coastal and oceanic currents that pass through the islands, as well as the warmer equatorial currents that are coursing beneath them, and this richness makes for abundant underwater life.

The islands straddle the equator nearly 1,000km (620miles) off the Ecuadorian coast of South America. It is the combination of the cold, plankton-rich waters and the warmer equatorial waters that allows a mix of temperate and tropical animals to exist. There are schools of big pelagic animals such as eagle rays, mantas, whales, and whale sharks that all rely on the plankton rich waters.

ABOVE: Diving with turtle

Costa Rica is better known for its aromatic coffee than for its diving opportunities, but the small island of Cocos, lying in isolation 480km (300miles) off the mainland Costa Rican coast, certainly makes up for it. It is an island that inspired a number of excellent yarns, such as Robert Louis Stevenson's *Treasure Island*, and although there are rumours of buried treasure, it hasn't yet been discovered. The most valuable treasures are probably to be found underwater! Since the days of swashbuckling pirates it has become a well-protected national park and is inhabited only by a handful of park rangers, along with a few pigs and some rats. Underwater, the currents are unrelenting but can make for an adrenalin-rush type of a dive, with sightings of hammerhead sharks, shoals of permit fish, white tip sharks, jacks, tuna, yellowtails and mackerel. This is also one of the few places in the world where you can still see giant sea turtles.

USEFUL INFORMATION

Climate: Equatorial, hot, but tends to be dry. Between November and June/July it is warmest, with temperatures of 29 and 30°C (84–86°F), the rest of the year it is about 23 or 24°C (72–74°F). Sea surface temperatures are between 24–27°C (74–80°F).

Currents: Moderate to strong.

Visibility: Fair to good.

Decompression chamber: No.

USEFUL INFORMATION

Water temperature: Generally a warm 28°C (82°F), and in the winter 26°C (79°F).

Climate: In the summer the average temperature is around 26°C (79°F), in the winter 24°C (74°F).

Currents: Strong.

Visibility: Good.

THE CAYMAN ISLANDS

If you imagine a mountain range such as the Andes that sits submerged under the Caribbean, you are some way to understanding the Cayman Islands – the islands are the tips of an enormous underwater mountain range. Grand Cayman, a prosperous centre for offshore finance, does not display this mountainous aspect however, and is completely flat, as is Little Cayman. Only Cayman Brac, the third island in the group, is slightly hilly. But as soon as you hit the water you have a more realistic perception of the lie of the land. Only a few metres from shore, the sea-bed, previously 10m (28ft) below you, suddenly disappears into the blue – five km (3miles) deep. On these sheer walls you can explore the

ABOVE: *Huge fan corals feed in the warm sea currents*

RIGHT: *Shoals of glass-fish catch everyone's eye*

canyons, gulleys, and check out the marine life that dwells there.

Grand Cayman, lying 780km (480miles) south of Miami, has an underwater landscape decorated with all types of sponge, and masses of black coral. Due to the depths that surround the island large schools of fish can be found, including schools of tarpon, some more than 200 strong. There are also wrecks, many of which probably sank during the numerous hurricanes that pass through this area.

Cayman Brac has a slightly more interesting array of creatures to show – there are strange hard corals, beautiful soft coral, groupers, schools of jacks, bright green moray eels, nurse sharks, and even schooling squid.

Little Cayman has canyons and crevices hiding a number of macro creatures. Cousteau once described the diving here as some of the best in the world, and it is here that you are most likely to see a manta ray too.

ABOVE: *Groupers get very big – but they're friendly!*

USEFUL INFORMATION

Water temperature: 26–27°C (79–80°F) in the summer, 25°C (78°F) in the winter.

Climate: Very warm and sunny. Temperatures of 30 and 31°C (86–88°F) in summer, 29°C (84°F) in winter.

Currents: Moderate.

Visibility: Good.

Decompression chamber: Yes.

THE BAHAMAS

The 700 islands of the Bahamas, off the east coast of Florida, are the epitome of paradise island existence. Here you will find beautiful coral reefs, with vertical drop-offs and underwater caverns to explore. The waters are so clear, it is not unusual to experience 50m (140ft) visibility and the Gulf Stream provides year-round warm water. There are plenty of shallow reefs lying close to shore, so you don't have to endure long boat journeys to reach good dive sites.

Some of the outer islands' reefs have been declared national parks, although the reefs are generally in good health everywhere. It is here, in the Bahamas, where you can sign up for a shark-feeding show. The shark-feeding dives are carefully controlled, and full instructions are given regarding how to behave. If the idea of a shark-feeding dive leaves your stomach churning, it may be best to go for the option of snorkelling or diving with dolphins instead, which are plentiful here. Or you could explore the 34m (112ft) freighter that was sunk near New Providence, at the northern end of the island chain, for the Bond film *Never Say Never Again*. Also off the coast of New Providence there is the chance to see pelagics, as depths here reach 2,500m (7000ft), creating good conditions for migration and feeding. Numerous coral reefs, walls and shipwrecks lie just offshore.

On the northerly Grand Bahama Island there are more than 100 identified dive sites. Over the centuries many ships have been wrecked around this island due to the shallow reefs, offering plenty of excitement for the wreck diver. Here too, you can experience shark diving or dolphin diving.

ABOVE: *Sponges are a world unto themselves*
RIGHT: *Snorkellers observe a forest of elkhorn coral*

On Abaco, the most northerly island in the Bahamas, there are more than 20 dive sites all within quick and easy reach of shore. Unlike some of the other islands, the dive centre staff here prefer not to hand-feed the sharks as some think this can lead to sharks associating humans with the food, leading to problems if there is, on occasion, no food to be had except for a tasty diver! So a chumsicle (50kg barrel of frozen bait) is thrown into the water and anchored to the sea-bed beneath the boat to attract sharks.

The largest but least populated of the Bahamian islands is Andros Island. With a landscape of pine forests, rivers, lakes, few roads and a couple of fishing villages, it is not a major tourist destination, but with a barrier reef which stretches 225km (140miles) along Andros' east coast, there is top-class diving to be found. The walls of the reef drop off to 2,000m (5660ft), and there are caverns, tunnels and blue holes to explore that have been formed by erosion in the limestone.

USEFUL INFORMATION

The water temperature is usually 26–27°C (79–81°F) in summer, and about 24°C (76°F) in winter.

Climate: In the summer the temperatures range from 27 to 31°C (81–88°F). In winter from 24 to 26°C (76–80°F).

Currents: Moderate.

Visibility: Good to excellent.

Decompression chamber: Yes.

BONAIRE

Bonaire is tiny island, just 40km (24miles) long and 8km (5miles) wide. It is one of the three islands which make up the Dutch Leeward islands: Aruba, Bonaire and Curacao, all of which are well known for their attractive landscapes and good diving. Situated on South America's north coast, the islands escape the hurricanes which often hit the Caribbean. Bonaire,

USEFUL INFORMATION

Water temperature: Usually between 26 and 27°C (76–80°F) in summer, 24 and 25°C (76–77°F) in winter.

Climate: October, November, and December are generally the wettest months. July and August have strong winds. Temperatures range from 27 and 30°C (80–86°F) in summer, 24 and 26°C (76–78°F) in winter.

Currents: Moderate.

Visibility: Good to excellent.

Decompression chamber: Yes.

ABOVE: Seahorses are very rare, very shy – but very beautiful

RIGHT Beneath the Old Town pier – one of the world's greatest shore-dives

BELOW: The arrowhead crab lives alongside the moray eel

although small, has a variety of landscapes for exploration: a pretty and hilly area to the north, a flat central section, and in the south there are sand dunes and mangrove swamps.

Due to its relatively sheltered position it provides good diving all year round. The water is clear and warm, and the reef surrounding the island was declared a marine park in 1979, making it illegal to spearfish, take corals, or to damage the corals in any way. Boats are also not allowed to drop anchor on the reef.

Thanks to the protection the reef has enjoyed, there is plenty to see underwater: large black grouper and tiger groupers are common, and schools of grey snapper and horse-eye jacks patrol the reef. There are large boulders, which combined with towers of star coral, make for a dramatic seascape. Further down the reef slope you can find delicate-looking sheet corals, where you may well see queen angelfish and other pretty reef fish.

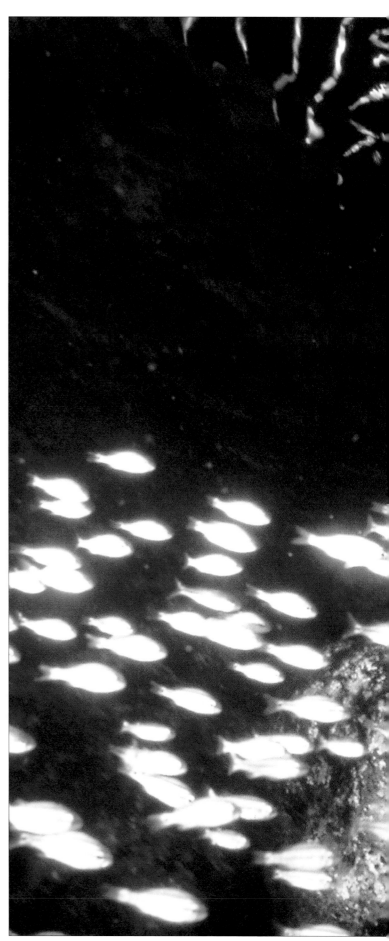

TOP LEFT: Christmas-tree worms can suddenly disappear when frightened

ABOVE: Featherstars cling to rocks in the warm tropical waters

RIGHT: Shoals of tiny fish congregate beneath old wooden piers

BERMUDA

Contrary to what Barry Manilo sings about Bermuda, you won't disappear as soon as you get there. It is made up of around 150 islands, of which the eight largest are connected by bridges and causeways, allowing residents to move from island to island. Only about 12 of the remaining islands are inhabited, which isn't so surprising when you realise that some of the 'islands' are just tiny clumps of rocks. Bermuda is one of the most isolated island groups in the world – it lies right in the middle of the North Atlantic. Luckily, the warm Gulf Stream passes by and creates a climate that is warm and almost tropical.

Despite being situated in the North Atlantic, Bermuda does have a coral reef system. The warm currents of the Gulf Stream nurture the corals and fish species, allowing rainbow parrotfish, angelfish, butterflyfish and other typical tropical reef dwellers to exist.

Bermuda is, of course, best known for the vast number of ships that have sunk there. This is probably due to the reef, which extends almost 13km (8miles) out to sea, and makes the area a navigational nightmare, as it is very shallow in places. There are estimates of the number of wrecks in the area that reach 150 and more. Most of these lie in water that is too deep to dive, but about 35 of them are accessible. These include a Spanish luxury liner, an American schooner, a Norwegian freighter, and an English barque. If you are lucky you may also spot a humpback whale, as they pass through during their annual migration northwards.

USEFUL INFORMATION

Water temperature: Usually two or three degrees lower than air temperature.

Climate: In summer (July–September) the average high is 29°C (84°F), the average low 24°C (74°F). January to March are the winter months, and the temperature then tends to range between 15.5 and 20.5°C (59–69°F). There is no rainy season.

Currents: Moderate to strong.

Visibility: Good.

Decompression chamber: Yes.

SCOTLAND

This is a land of folklore, legends and myths such as the Loch Ness monster. Scotland encompasses many islands, sea lochs and dramatic mountain scenery. It has a beautiful landscape with a sky that changes every time you look away and back again. With a coastline (including islands and sea lochs) that is more than 10,000km (6500miles) long, it is no wonder that there is a wide-ranging variety of dive sites available. Diving Scotland's coastline can be a wonderful, if unusual, diving experience – the underwater life is exceptionally profuse, there are many exciting wrecks, and the underwater cliffs and spooky caves can take your breath away. Scotland is probably best known among divers, for Scapa Flow, where there are possibly more shipwrecks than any other location on the planet. It is a deep, cold natural harbour that served the warring nations' fleets for centuries. Many considered it to be impregnable to attack as it is sheltered by a protective ring of islands. In 1919, when the German Imperial Fleet was captured and confined in the bay, Admiral Ludwig von Reuter believed his fleet was to be used against his own people, so to save further embarrassment he deliberately sunk the fleet, without knowing that an armistice had

BELOW: Scallops are good to look at, as well as eat!

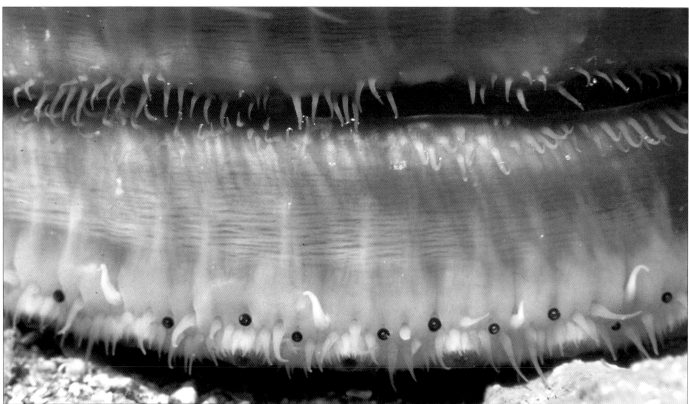

already been agreed. The bulk of the wrecks in Scapa Flow are made up of this fleet. Ships were also sunk deliberately as 'block ships' to stop access into the bay by enemy ships. There are three battleships, four light cruisers, five torpedo boats (destroyers), a World War II destroyer, two submarines, 27 large sections of remains and salvors' equipment, 16 known British wrecks, 32 block ships, and two battleships. A further 54 wrecks are yet to be identified.

Loch Fyne is another excellent dive location. It is part of an ancient fault-line which continues up into the Scottish Highlands and due to its long and sheltered nature, can be dived at any time of the year. The shores of the Loch are, in general, steep sloping, and there are cliffs that drop down to depths of 20m (66ft). Basking sharks can be seen in the lower regions of the loch in the summer, but these gentle giants are rarely seen by divers. With or without a basking shark sighting, the loch has plenty for divers to see, including lobsters, large dahlia anemones, brightly-coloured sponges and sea squirts, scallops, starfish and brittle stars.

LEFT: The wrecks of Scapa Flow support all kinds of creatures

BELOW: Eye-to-eye with a fiercely territorial crab

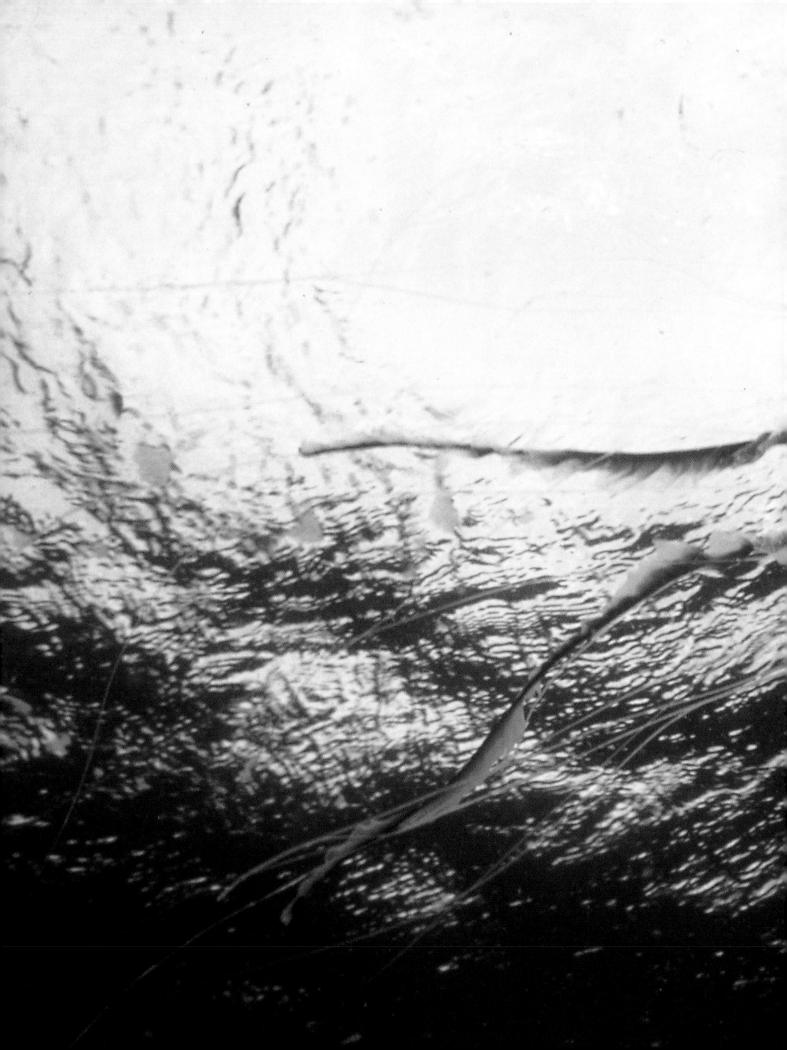

ABOVE: Hungry jewel anemones searching for food

USEFUL INFORMATION

Water temperature: Average at 7.5°C (45°F) in February, 9°C (48°F) in May, 13°C (54°F) in August and 10.5°C (51°F) in November.

Climate: In Scotland, summer temperatures may reach the mid-twenties, but it is more likely to be a chilly 18 or 19°C (64–66°F).
The water is usually 12 or 13°C (54–55°F) in the summer, and 6 or 7°C (41–44°F) in the winter. Most of Ireland is warmer than Scotland, and so the temperatures are likely to be a few degrees higher.

Currents: Moderate.

Visibility: Good to excellent.

Decompression chamber: Yes (both Scotland and Ireland).

IRELAND

Diving in Ireland is refreshingly different – there is dramatic underwater scenery, colourful anemones, many species of shellfish and invertebrates, and then, on the larger scale, there are seals, dolphins and basking sharks. On the Atlantic coastlines the visibility can reach 40m (130ft), although it is more usually in the 15 – 20m (50 – 66ft) range. The water is incredibly clean and unpolluted, as is indicated by the large quantities of sea urchins, crustaceans and fish. But it is not just for its marine life that the Irish coast is renown – there are estimated hundreds of wrecks long the Cork coastline, many of which are at diveable depths.

5
UNDERWATER ACTIVITIES

ABOVE: Sunken wrecks offer exciting opportunities for dramatic underwater photography

NIGHT DIVING

Diving at night offers a new experience and the opportunity to see the underwater environment from a different perspective. One of the greatest attractions of night diving is the chance of encountering nocturnal marine animals, seldom seen during the day. Behavioural patterns too can be seen to change dramatically as predators emerge and almost a sense of panic descends on a reef. Diving a familiar site at night can add a sense of mystery; many divers have observed a ghostly feeling when diving a shipwreck at night.

EQUIPMENT REQUIREMENTS

At the very least a night diver should carry a primary light with a wide or 'umbrella' beam, and a back-up light. Typically, the back-up light may be smaller so it can be securely fastened out of the way unless it is needed. In the event of a primary light failure (unless a second powerful light is available), a night dive should be aborted. Back-up lights are only used to safely ascend to the surface and exit the water, and therefore need not be so powerful. Many divers carry more than one back-up light in case both lights fail or a buddy requires one. A useful tip is to turn the torch on before entering the water and keep it on until exiting the water.

Strobe beacons that flash intermittently or chemical glow sticks are used to indicate current position both while diving and upon surfacing. These may be secured to a part of the BCD, regulator hoses or the diving cylinder. They may also be attached to a surface marker buoy for surface support crew to watch, or used to mark an ascent line or even the dive boat.

Many divers carry a whistle or some other audio signalling device to alert boats to their position in the dark.

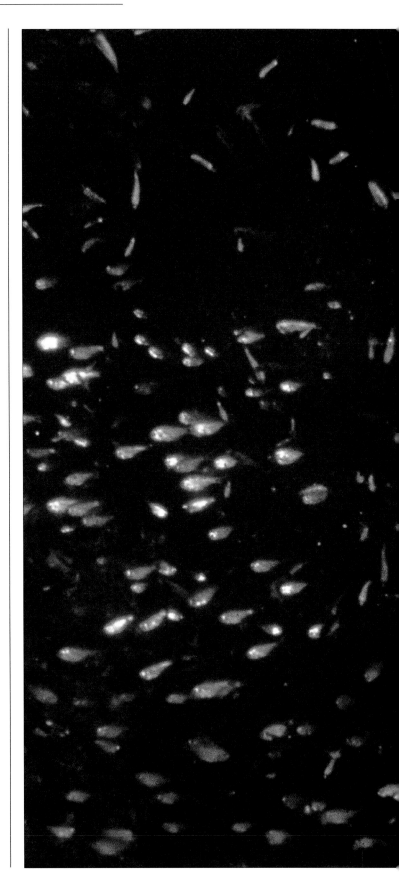

RIGHT: The reef plays host to different critters at night

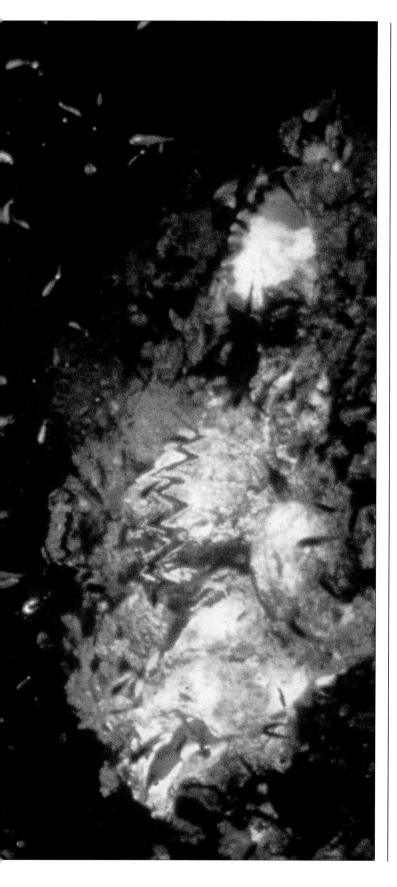

RULES FOR NIGHT DIVING

● As visibility at night, even in the clearest waters, is limited to the edges of your torch beam, it is important to be familiar with any chosen dive site. Dive it first during the day, taking note of navigational references you could use later for orientation. Remember, the more familiar you are with your chosen route, the less likely you will get lost. While ascending from a dive early because you are lost should not be dangerous, it can be frustrating, and may tempt you to re-descend, increasing the risk of decompression sickness.

● Choosing carefully who you dive with and the equipment you use may also increase the enjoyment of night diving. Regular buddies are often easier to recognise and communicate with underwater than a new diving partner. They will also be familiar with the equipment you use and how to operate it. In return you should know your own kit and pay careful attention to your buddies during a pre-dive equipment check. Ensuring that important safety items, such as alternate air sources, are well positioned and correctly configured will make them easier to find in the dark.

COMMUNICATING ON A NIGHT DIVE

Using conventional underwater communication techniques can sometimes be difficult at night. Instead, divers rely heavily on artificial (torch) light for simple signalling. Circling with the torch beam indicates everything is okay, while briefly waving the torch beam from side to side is used to gain attention. Continued waving of the torch is an indication of distress. Alternatively, a diver may use their torch beam to highlight conventional hand signals in front of their chest.

At the surface, signalling to a party on the shore can also be difficult. Again, making a circular motion with the torch beam signals 'okay'. Alternatively, a diver may raise their arm and point the torch light downwards, at the top of their head, signalling 'okay'. Making a waving motion, even briefly, at the surface indicates distress.

WRECK DIVING

For many divers the chance to explore sunken wrecks is one of the big attractions of the sport. Wrecks hold a history all of their own and offer one of the most exciting and atmospheric underwater activities.

Wreck diving can be split into two different categories: recreational and advanced wreck diving. While there is a definite division between the two, any wreck diving requires special training.

Recreational wreck diving is undertaken within maximum recreational depth and time limits, and involves little or no penetration of the wreck. Advanced wreck diving is anything that requires maximum recreational depth or time limits be exceeded and/or involves entry inside the wreck.

ABOVE: Wrecks generate a powerful attraction for scuba-divers

EQUIPMENT REQUIREMENTS

In general, recreational wreck diving can be undertaken safely with no additional equipment. To maximise enjoyment, however, it is often best to carry a torch to light up areas of the wreck shaded from natural light.

Advanced penetration wreck diving can be more hazardous so requires the use of appropriate safety equipment. As well as a primary light it is often wise to carry at least one additional back-up.

It is common practice to carry a reel with a 15–30m (50–100 ft) line, marking out a clear route from point of entry inside a wreck, that may be traced back to ensure a safe exit.

RULES FOR WRECK DIVING

● Assess all wreck dives before undertaking them and never embark on a dive that requires levels of skill and experience beyond your personal limits. While wrecks are often regarded as a divers' playground, they can be potential death traps, so ensure all your wreck dives are carefully planned and stick to predetermined routes to maximise safety. Make sure your buddy is informed when planning each dive. If they intend to enter a wreck and you are not trained to do so or simply don't feel like it, let them know; neither of you should then penetrate the wreck.

● Diving on any wreck is a privilege that should not be abused. Never remove parts of a wreck or items from it as souvenirs. No matter how small or insignificant they may seem, they should be left for all to enjoy. Wrecks also form artificial reefs. If you lift away part of a wreck you may actually be destroying a home.

ABOVE: A torch is essential to stay in contact with your buddy

DEEP DIVING

Recreational, deep, extended range diving is generally classed as any dive below 30 to 40m (100–130ft). The exact definition varies from one agency to another. Some training bodies practise deep decompression diving, while others such as PADI, who don't teach any decompression diving, stay within no-decompression limits.

Deep 'technical' diving is any dive beyond recreational limits, requiring high levels of skill and experience. Many of the world's most experienced technical divers are reaching depths in excess of 100 metres (330ft); this cannot reasonably be covered in this book. Anyone interested in diving below recreational limits should look to recognised technical training agencies for further advice.

BELOW: Diver with double tanks

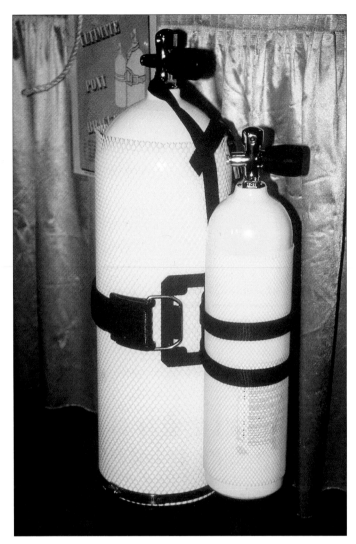

ABOVE: Safety first – a pony cylinder makes deep dives more comfortable

EQUIPMENT REQUIREMENTS

It is vital that any deep diving activity is undertaken with all the appropriate equipment. With the exception of physiological concerns, deep divers are restricted most by the amount of breathing gas they carry; there must be enough gas to make decompression or safety stops and ascend with at least 50 bar of pressure remaining. Even a short dive to 30m (100ft) would dictate the use of a 12–litre cylinder filled to pressures of 300 bar or a 15–litre, 232 bar. Many divers also carry a redundant alternative gas source, such as a three-litre side-slung pony bottle, providing a completely independent supply. A dive of 40 to 50m (130–165ft) would dictate more primary gas be carried, so often cylinders are 'twinned' together. Deep technical diving beyond 50 to 60m (200ft) requires the use of multiple cylinders. A typical set-up may include back mounted twin 12-litre tanks and two side-slung seven or ten-litre

'stage cylinders'. Often cylinders are hung on lines from the surface at agreed decompression or safety stop depths, providing additional breathing gas should it be required.

As well as choosing the correct selection of tanks, deep divers must look at using other appropriate kit. Any arrangement of more than one cylinder will require the use of a rugged BCD with a high lift capacity. High performance regulators should also be used when deep diving. To counter low light levels it is generally advised that a powerful torch is carried. It is also often necessary to wear a warmer exposure suit as lower water temperatures are experienced at depth. Some deep divers also carry a spare mask that can be worn, should a strap break.

ABOVE: The sunlight penetrates deep into tropical waters

WHY DEEP DIVERS DON'T ALWAYS BREATHE AIR

There are many physiological hazards encountered when deep diving. Increased risk of DCS as high levels of nitrogen are absorbed is a constant factor. Nitrogen narcosis, while simple to cure, is ever present at depth. Divers must remain aware that the increased partial pressure of oxygen can cause it to become toxic at depth. To combat these problems, divers select different mixtures of gases to breathe, depending on depth.

A common practice is to increase the percentage of oxygen beyond 21 per cent, creating an oxygen-rich gas. The gas pro-duced may be referred to as 'Nitrox' or 'Enriched Air'. While div-ing with a higher percentage of oxygen slows down nitrogen absorption and therefore the risk of DCS, it increases the risk of oxygen toxicity. So, contrary to popular belief, a diver using Nitrox, to dive safely, must stay at shallower depths than a diver breathing air. For this reason recreational deep divers may use air as a 'bottom gas' and breathe Nitrox at the end of a dive, in shallower water, when decompressing or making safety stops. This eliminates nitrogen at a faster rate than air, reducing the risk of DCS.

Using Nitrox requires the use of special training and special-ly modified equipment to avoid potential hazards. As a high oxy-gen mixture can react with other substances and burn or explode, diving cylinders and regulators must be oxygen cleaned by a qualified service technician.

Other gases such as helium are used by deep technical divers. They require special training and cannot reasonably be explained in this book.

Above: Fan corals

RULES FOR DEEP DIVING

- Choose an experienced buddy, ensuring they are trained in deep diving techniques. Run through every part of the dive at the surface first, checking hand signals and re-checking both your own and your buddy's equipment.

- All deep dives require careful planning and execution. As bottom times are often short, it is important to be well pre-pared and undertake your chosen route immediately upon reaching the desired depth. Always descend to your maximum intended depth and work your way gradually shallower, never re-descending; this will mean you continually gas off nitrogen. You will most likely experience some form of narcosis, so remain alert and well disciplined, continually monitoring depth and time limits.

- Begin preparing to ascend before you reach the agreed max-imum time limit. It usually takes a minute or so to signal and actually start ascending; you don't want to exceed limits. Keep your ascent rate slow but continuous, until you reach decom-pression or safety stop depth. If you do ever exceed a time or depth limit add extra time to your stop to decrease the chance of DCS.

CAVERN AND CAVE DIVING

For many divers, exploring caverns and caves is a unique diving activity. Networks of tunnels and huge open rooms offer a unique environment for the adventurous diver. Training agencies simply and clearly define the difference between a cavern and a cave A cavern is an area penetrated by sunlight, a cave is not.

Cavern diving is generally regarded as an advanced recreational diving activity. All divers must complete numerous cavern dives before making a cave dive. As cave networks can be very narrow, it is vital a diver understands fully all the correct procedures.

Cave diving is a highly specialised technical diving activity and should not be attempted by recreational cavern divers.

Above: Training is crucial for cavern divers

EQUIPMENT REQUIREMENTS

Most well-equipped recreational divers will own most of the required kit for making basic cavern dives. It may, however, be necessary to make minor modifications to ensure safety and enjoyment.

It is agreed among cavers both on land and underwater that at least three reliable lights should be carried at all times: one primary light and two back-ups. For recreational cavern divers it is usually only necessary to carry one.

In any environment where it may not be possible to make a direct ascent to the surface, it is important to ensure that alternative air sources are easy to locate and use. Many cavern and cave divers prefer to use 1.5 or 2m (6.5ft) hoses attached to their alternative air sources. These longer hose lengths make it much easier to share air during an emergency exit through a confined space: the diver receiving the alternative air source can swim directly behind the donor. Long hoses can be tucked under elastic or rubber bands fitted to the diving cylinder.

A safety line carried on a lightweight reel is an essential item of equipment for a cavern or cave diver. Bad visibility is a commonly encountered problem, even in large caverns,

as divers stir up sediment with their fins. The use of a line to indicate an exit route is therefore a must. While some regularly dived caverns may have lines already laid out for divers to simply clip themselves onto, most require a safety line be laid out from the entrance, as a diver passes through. Brightly coloured markers can be bought and attached to lines, making them clearly visible, even in poor light.

Besides these additional considerations, it is vital that all equipment is well configured and closely secured to minimise the risk of entanglement. Spare torches and reels might be attached to D-rings or stored in a BCD pocket. Snorkels should not be used as they can become snagged. A spare mask should be carried in case it is needed.

RIGHT: Tuck long hose under elastic bands on the diving cylinder

ABOVE: It is essential to carry a spare mask when cavern diving mask

ABOVE: Diver connected to alternative air source by long hose

ABOVE: If you're going into his cave, don't step on him!

RULES FOR CAVERN AND CAVE DIVING

● All cavern and cave dives must be well planned. Detailed preparation at the surface before entering any overhead environment is the key to a safe, successful dive. Your planning should include appropriate buddy team selection; an ideal dive team should be composed of divers of similar experience and ability. This factor more than anything else must dictate your overall dive objective.

● The amount of breathing gas you carry will dictate the distance it is possible to penetrate inside a cave or cavern. Dive by the rule of thirds: after you have used a third of your gas, turn around and begin heading back out of the cavern or cave. You should use a third of your gas getting back to the exit, leaving a third in reserve, for safety.

● As a rule, when diving caverns or basic caves, use one line only. Penetrate only as far as your line will allow, then turn around and make your exit.

Agree on any methods of communication prior to entering the water. A common practice is for every diver to keep one hand on the line and use a differing number of light 'tugs' to communicate.

● Remember, cave diving should be regarded as a technical diving activity, requiring levels of training and knowledge beyond that taught on a recreational cavern diving course.

SCOOTER DIVING

Scooter diving is an exhilarating way to travel underwater. Many resorts offer rental scooters or diver propulsion vehicles (DPVs) and offer classes on using them safely. Scooters are battery powered submersibles that tow the diver behind them. They are easy to fly with just a little practice and are guided by pointing the nose where you want to go.

Scooters are often used just for fun. But they also have serious applications. With cameras mounted on board they may be used to film fast moving animals like whale sharks or to survey large areas such as wrecks. They may also be used for underwater searches and to excavate in sand, mud or silt by aiming the propeller at the sea floor.

ABOVE: When exploring beneath an overhead environment, scooters can be useful

EQUIPMENT REQUIREMENTS

Scooters are available in different configurations. Recreational units are normally constructed from plastics and depth-rated to 40m (130ft). On a single charge they will typically run for 40 to 80 minutes and cover 2–3km (1.25–1.8miles). Most can operate at several speeds. Lower speeds provide longer running times while higher speeds reduce it. Scooters aimed at technical and professional divers are usually aluminium and much heavier than recreational models. They may have ranges of 4km (2.5miles) or more. Professional scooters can operate below 100m (330ft). Long-range scooters are designed to be straddled and may be steered using bow planes.

Scooter diving places tremendous strain on the pilot's arms because of drag from bulky scuba equipment. To prevent this, some scooters use a bridle that clips the vehicle to the divers harness. Others have a fixed T-bar on the stern that sits behind the thighs.

To navigate and for depth control an instrument panel is usually fitted. Some DPVs have battery life indicators to help the diver judge how much farther he can travel.

In case a scooter floods or needs to be jettisoned and recovered later, it is good practice to attach a small, easily deployed lifting bag or buoy to the vehicle.

RULES FOR SCOOTER DIVING

● It is easy to get carried away on a DPV. Their speed and manoevreability encourages aquabatics like close passes, barrel rolls, inverted flying and somersaults. Collisions and lung expansion injuries are a frequent occurrence. It is also easy to stray far from the shore or your boat and be unable to return if the unit is damaged or batteries fail.

● For safety one should only normally fly a DPV for one third of its range, allowing you one third for the return journey and a comfortable safety zone. You should remain within easy swimming range of the shore or have a boat accompany you in case your DPV stops working or you have to abandon it. Build in a larger than normal air reserve – by eliminating swimming you'll find your air lasts far longer. If you have to swim back you need sufficient air to counter the massively increased workload.

● Most DPVs can tow two divers making it simple to maintain the buddy system. If flying a pair of DPVs, it is easy to pull ahead of or fall behind your buddy and become separated. Be extra vigilant to prevent this.

● Flying DPVs is addictive, but requires special training to be both fun and safe.

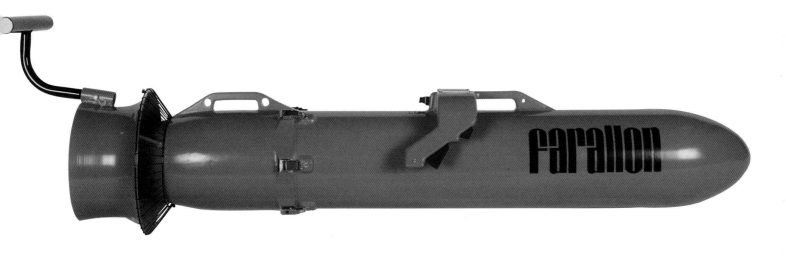

ABOVE: Scooter (or DPV), streamlined for speed

REBREATHER DIVING

Rebreather diving is an emerging form of recreational and technical diving. Rebreathers emit few bubbles making them quieter than ordinary scuba and because they reuse most of the breathing gas, much more efficient and economical.

EQUIPMENT REQUIREMENTS

Semi Closed Rebreathers (SCRs) typically use Nitrox and are mechanically controlled. They consist of a breathing bag or counterlung into which the diver inhales and exhales, scrubbers which remove carbon dioxide from the exhaled air before it re-enters the counterlung to be breathed again, and a gas bottle to top up the breathing gas from time to time. Because they do not re-use all of the divers exhaled air, periodically they exhaust bubbles. However there are fewer bubbles than with ordinary scuba.

Close Circuit Rebreathers (CCRs) also have a counterlung and scrubber system. However, on board electronic computers are used to mix gases from several cylinders. One contains oxygen, the other a diluent, such as helium. Because they recycle all of the exhaled gas, CCRs only exhaust bubbles during the ascent. This makes them virtually silent and perfect for underwater film makers and photographers who need to get close to shy animals. For diving to great depths using expensive gases like helium closed circuit rebreathers are more economical than open circuit scuba because almost no gas is lost during the dive. Less gas needs to be carried and may be used for several dives.

RULES FOR REBREATHER DIVING

- Using rebreathers is very different to using open circuit scuba. Far more training and experience is required to use them safely. They also require far more attention during the dive and considerably greater maintenance so that they remain safe to use.

- Because rebreather failures are likely to be catastrophic, some form of bail-out system needs to be used. Some rebreathers have double or even triple redundancy, meaning that if a critical component fails, there's at least one and possibly two back-ups to take its place.

- Proper training is absolutely essential for safe rebreather diving. Currently the technology is so new in the recreational and technical diving fields that few people have much experience of using them for any great length of time. Rebreather manufacturers require purchasers to undergo training before buying their own units. Even so, some rebreathers have been used by individuals for dives beyond their training level with tragic results.

ABOVE: Training is crucial before using a rebreather

UNDERWATER IMAGING

It is only natural that those who enjoy diving want to show non-diving friends and colleagues what attracts them to the sport. The easiest way is through underwater photography or underwater videography.

EQUIPMENT REQUIREMENTS

For stills photography either an underwater camera or a land camera in a housing can be used. Underwater cameras range from single-use cameras, costing just a few pounds that can be used in shallow water, through to professional cameras costing thousands. Housings are made for simple throwaway cameras through to the most sophisticated professional models.

Simple cameras work best in clear, well-lit water. They will provide snap shots in good conditions. However, if the water is murky, using a camera with a built-in flash creates backscatter – particles of dirt in the water are lit by the flash and it looks as if the pictures were taken through snow.

To avoid this, a camera with a detachable flash or strobe must be used. This lets you angle the gun to avoid backscatter and also lets you use creative lighting effects. Because such cameras are bulky, they are best suited to divers with a genuine interest in underwater photography who are diving in order to take pictures.

For serious underwater photographers, a modern land camera in a housing offers the benefits of autofocus and allows the use of a range of specialist lenses. These features make them adaptable to almost any shooting situation.

Underwater videographers use normal camcorders inside waterproof housings. These range from 'bag housings' for shallow diving to professional aluminium housings for semi-professional and broadcast use. Hi8, VHS-C, Mini DV and DV are the most popular camcorders as they can be placed in small lightweight housings for travelling.

Video lights on arms are used to provide illumination under dark conditions or at night and to restore colours. Some videographers use special colour correction filters instead for daylight recording.

An advantage of video is that it can be replayed immediately after a dive so that mistakes can be corrected and to provide a guide as to what additional sequences need to be shot.

RULES FOR UNDERWATER IMAGING

● The greatest risk in shooting stills or video underwater is becoming distracted. The excitement of following a subject like a manta ray makes it easy to lose track of depth, time and air. It is also very easy to either lose your buddy or not notice that they need assistance.

● Because successful underwater imaging requires concentration on the camera and the subject, personal diving skills must be excellent. If your diving skills are weak they will distract you from your photography. It is essential to be a well-trained and experienced diver before attempting underwater imaging.

● Care for the environment is crucial. Precision buoyancy control is vital to proper camera handling and avoidance of damaging coral or kicking up silt. Smooth, fluid movements disturb marine animals less than jerky ones and make them more approachable resulting in better images. Manipulating subjects is intrusive, may endanger the animal and invites criticism when the picture is published or video screened.

ABOVE: This underwater photographer uses a land camera in a special housing

ICE DIVING

Diving under ice can be captivating. Ice formations can be very beautiful and the opportunity exists to observe creatures that are found nowhere else but under the Arctic and Antarctic icecaps. In less exotic places diving under ice merely extends the diving season.

EQUIPMENT FOR ICE DIVING

Ice diving is a highly specialised activity requiring suitably specialised equipment. The cold conditions place additional demands on the diver and his equipment. Exposure to the extreme cold means that dry suits are normally chosen. Specially modified regulators are used that resist freezing, which can either cause the valve to freeflow or lock up, shutting off the air supply. A secondary air source is normally carried as additional protection, as the diver will have to return to the entry hole before he can surface if the primary air supply fails. Instruments must be suited to cold water use – some depth gauges are not and can provide misleading depth information. Harnesses are used to connect the diver to the surface via a lifeline.

RULES FOR ICE DIVING

● The main risk in ice diving is becoming lost under the ice cap and running out of air before the entry hole is located. To avoid this a diver is always roped to the surface via a life line. The end of the line is secured so that it cannot possibly be dragged into the entry hole and lost. A designated tender looks after the lifeline, and rope signals can be used for communication between tender and diver. A strobe or bright object like a bucket is often hung below the entry hole to provide a visual marker if the line does become lost and a 'wheel' is marked on the ice surface around the hole. A lost diver can see this from under the water and follow the 'spokes' back to the hole and safety. A standby diver remains kitted up next to the hole in case of emergency. He can enter the water instantly, trailing his own lifeline to begin a search if required.

● Ice diving should be conducted only by divers who have been trained by a certified ice diving instructor.

RIGHT: Planning the dive and successfully executing the plan is the ultimate goal of the ice-diver

6

AQUATIC REALM

The biological complexity of the marine environment – of which divers get a relatively small glimpse – is astounding, and seemingly boundless. All the marine plants and most of the animals live in the upper 1,000m (0.6mile) of the oceans. Life began in the sea, and even today there are many marine species that have never evolved terrestrial counterparts.

Fish appeared approximately 350 million years ago, while other famous inhabitants of the sea, such as whales, are newcomers, having moved into the marine environment from the land about 60 million years ago. Primitive humans first harvested food from the sea about a million years ago, and only began seriously exploring the underwater world in the last 50 years.

This chapter will consider the environments regularly explored by divers, as well as the creatures we are likely to encounter. The invention of scuba apparatus has enabled an unprecedented number of people to explore the upper layers of our oceans in recent years. Ironically, the breakthrough has come at a time when the same technological society is posing the biggest-ever threat to the aquatic realm.

BELOW: A rare treat: divers swim with a whale shark

MANTA RAYS AND WHALE SHARKS:
Gentle giants

Two of the world's most awe-inspiring sea creatures have become the twin holy grails of tropical scuba diving: the manta ray and the whale shark. The whale shark (*rhincodon typus*) is the world's largest fish, and it can easily be recognised by its size. The head is flat and ends in a large mouth that filters tons of plankton-rich water every day. These behemoths can grow to a length of 18m (60ft), but are completely non-aggressive and occasionally show interest in divers and snorkelers. It prefers to swim near the surface where it feeds on small fish, cephalopods and crustaceans.

Experienced divers can go through an entire lifetime without encountering one of these pelagic wanderers, but they make guaranteed appearances off the coast of Madagascar and Ningaloo Reef, Western Australia, during coral spawnings. Swimming alongside a whale shark is an almost transcendental experience, but take care to avoid the pendulous sweeps of the tail. A hefty blow, albeit an accident, could ruin your entire trip. Some countries now run whale shark tagging programmes to monitor these seldom-seen fish, as there are fears that shark fisheries may be depleting the whale shark population in the Indian Ocean.

The manta *(manta birostris)* is the largest member of the ray family, and can attain lengths of 6m (20ft) across its vast pectoral fins. Also a filter feeder, it is usually wary of divers but occasionally shows signs of curiosity and even friendliness. Apart from its sheer size, the manta can be distinguished by a pair of long, flat cephalic fins, separated by the long arch of the mouth. These are used to funnel plankton-rich water into the mouth. Large groups of these so-called devilfish are regularly seen off the Micronesian island of Yap, where they swoop down to the reef to have their bodies cleaned of parasites by obliging angelfish.

But the largest and friendliest mantas are to be found around Mexico's Revillagegidos Islands, where many divers have been literally swept off their feet by huge rays eager to give them a free ride. Such experiences are not common, but have earned a worthy place in diving lore.

RIGHT: Manta ray, just off Revillagegidos Islands, Mexico

In general, the best advice for a diver who wants to get close to a manta is to let the ray come to you. Chasing mantas is folly: they've spent a few hundred million years evolving the ideal form for sustained swimming, and you've got a pair of fins. No contest. Instead, why not rely on the intelligence and curiosity of the creature (biologists believe they are probably about as intelligent as a cat). If you do not present a threat, it will be better disposed to investigating you. Some mantas have even discovered the joys of a good Jacuzzi, and deliberately hover above a diver so that his or her bubbles gently massage their wings

BELOW: Whale shark with rare bait wall

DOLPHINS AND WHALES

Dolphins are now regarded as second only to humans in terms of raw intellect. They are increasingly viewed as having mystical healing powers, although there is absolutely no evidence for this.

Whales are equally popular, though they are only just beginning to make a recovery after years of commercial slaughter. They are certainly among the most impressive creatures in the sea: the blue whale is the largest animal ever; the humpback undertakes the longest migrations and sings the most complex songs; the sperm whale is the ocean's largest predator and is believed to be able to dive deeper than any other mammal.

The cetacean family is unofficially divided into whales, dolphins and porpoises, but the words have no real scientific basis and cause confusion. For instance, the famous killer whale is actu-ally a large dolphin (some people prefer to call them orcas). It is more accurate to think of cetaceans in two groups: toothed whales and baleen whales, which filter the sea for food.

Scuba divers regard a meeting with any cetacean as a rare privilege, but strict protocol should be observed in such a situation, especially the 'no-touching' rule. It is worth bearing in mind that many cetaceans exhale bubbles as a sign of irritation. A group of scuba divers, constantly belching noisy air, must present an unsettling picture. It is a testimony to the animals' intelligence and patience that they ever bother with us at all!

There are no guarantees and no scheduled appearances with wild dolphins: they come and swim with you if they feel like it. Increasingly, people are searching out these experiences and as is inevitable, there have been reports of boats harassing dolphins and ignoring guidelines. It is the responsibility of every diver to ensure that everyone, from fellow divers to boat operators, keeps to the

BELOW: Common dolphins in the Azores.

rules. Here are a few tips for an encounter that will please not just the human, but the dolphin as well.

- *Keep your arms by your side when you swim.*
- *Take an underwater toy like a hoop, but don't wave it around in an aggressive manner.*
- *Be very careful if you are using an underwater scooter. Dolphins sometimes like to swim together with them, and do not appreciate collisions.*
- *Do not feed the dolphins, as it changes their behaviour and makes them vulnerable to disease.*
- *Baby dolphins are fun to be with because they are extremely curious. But back off immediately if the mother shows signs of irritation (snaps her jaws, blows bubbles, and swims erratically).*

The view of dolphins as cute and cuddly is misleading (they bully other cetaceans and even commit infanticide and rape their own species), but they remain undiminished as ambassadors of the sea. For humans, they represent a chance to learn the workings of a sophisticated animal society with alliances and rivalries as complex as our own system.

For divers, there is nothing to match the full-on adrenaline rush of a face-to-face encounter with a huge whale in its own habitat. This is usually best achieved using snorkelling gear, as silence and manoeuvrability are more important than breathing apparatus (if the whales want to dive, chances are they will go rather deeper than recreational scuba limits).

Snorkelling is permitted with the humpback whales that congregate in the Silver Banks of the Bahamas every summer. It is sometimes possible to swim right up to a mother as she is tending her calf, but be careful not to annoy the adults by harassing their youngsters. Pilot whales and various types of dolphin are occasionally encountered by swimmers off the coasts of Atlantic islands like the Azores and the Canaries.

But the ultimate encounter, and one which is definitely not for the inexperienced, is a swim with an adult sperm whale (not a bull, if you value your life), an animal which could swallow a human as easily as a peanut. Such interactions have taken place in the Azores, although at the time of writing the issue was controversial, and the government was considering moves to regulate whale watching and stop snorkelling with the mammals. These days, whales need protection from people who just love them too much.

LEFT: The reef is beautiful, but watch the blue for unexpected visitors

CORAL REEFS

Of all the images of paradise on Earth, nothing seems as fitting as that of a thriving coral reef. Coral reefs are among the most beautiful and diverse gardens of life on our planet. The solid, rooted structures do not appear animal in origin, but they are. Coral reefs are composed of the brittle, calcified structures of tiny creatures called polyps, which have built on each other, generation after generation. The process takes many years, but it has produced great wonders like the atolls of Maldives and the world's largest natural structure, the Great Barrier Reef of northeast Australia.

There are two important factors in the life cycle of coral: sunlight and clean water. The coral polyps extend their tentacles into the passing currents to strain out plankton, on which they feed. They need the sun and the process of photosynthesis to facilitate the growth of symbiotic algae that give them the oxygen and lime they need to make their skeletons. Coral communities have proved uniquely adaptable to man's nautical errors, and have used countless shipwrecks as solid foundations on which to build structures. They literally turn death into life.

ABOVE: The vibrant colours of a healthy reef

ABOVE: An oriental sweetlips patrols a reef

Coral reefs protect the lands they surround from ocean storms and provide homes for millions of fish and invertebrates. Complex food chains have evolved thanks to the existence of such reefs, which attract large ocean-going fish like jacks and tuna. Larger predators such as sharks prey on these in turn.

For divers, coral reefs are simply a joy to behold. The most colourful and interesting parts of the reef are usually within safe diving depth, and many offer protection from potentially danger-ous ocean currents. Reefs can be close to the surface or sub-merged, and may be sloping or even vertical. Many divers say there is nothing to compare to the thrill of swimming alongside a sheer wall of coral dropping off into oblivion.

Fringing reefs are inshore and tend to suffer more from land-based processes that can limit visibility. Some of the best reefs are submerged in open water washed by tides or currents. Divers who want to visit such sites should be in sound physical shape and should have reasonably advanced skills, as well as the

confidence to descend as quickly as possible through the surface current, to the shelter of the reef. The reward is a fecund reef with attractions such as sharks, barracuda and large schools of fish.

Although every coral reef is unique in some way, the types of coral and fish encountered in the Caribbean are noticeably dif-ferent from their Indo-Pacific cousins (although there are many common species). Caribbean reefs have been described as ornate but restrained gardens compared to the multi-coloured coral jungles of the Pacific. Still, every reef has its emblem, from the inquisitive Napoleon wrasse of the Red Sea to the grotesque Merlot's scorpionfish of Papua New Guinea. For the diver, there are countless worlds to be discovered and new creatures to be documented in virgin reefs. Who knows what oddities are wait-ing out there, beyond the limits of visibility and imagination?

In 1997 and 1998, marine biologists reported unprecedented levels of a destructive phenomenon known as coral bleaching in some of the world's most famous snorkelling and diving resorts, brought on by abnormally high water temperatures. The National Oceanic and Atmospheric Administration of America received reports of massive levels of coral bleaching at sites in the Great Barrier Reef, French Polynesia, Kenya, the Galapagos Islands, Florida Keys, Baja California, the Yucatan Coast, Cayman Islands and the Dutch Antilles.

The widespread damage to reefs was another by-product of El Niño, the warming of the Pacific's surface waters which regularly causes havoc across the planet with its various climactic side-effects.

The most serious bleaching took place in the Maldives, where swimming up some previously fecund reefs was likened to ascending a snow-capped Alpine landscape.

Coral bleaching occurs as a result of microscopic algae that live in symbiosis with the coral tissue – zooxanthellae – being expelled due to stress. Corals are highly sensitive to heat changes, and react badly if they encounter changes of just a few degrees Celsius, even for a matter of days.

Bleaching does not necessarily kill coral but it does hurt the organism. Although the coral can survive for a while on its own and recover from the bleaching, lengthy temperature abnormal-ities (periods of more than two weeks) such as those caused by the 1997/1998 El Niño can result in death.

It remains unclear how much of a departure from the norm this event really was, and what implications it holds for the future of our tropical reefs.

SHARKS

Visitors to the aquatic realm can be separated into two distinct groups: those who would rather die than come face-to-face with a shark, and those who would sell their souls for such an encounter. Today's sharks, represented by more than 350 known species and others still waiting to be discovered, are the result of a process of evolution 250 million years in the making.

The undisputed king of sharks is the great white, or white pointer, found throughout the world's temperate seas but mostly off the coasts of California, South Africa and south Australia. The shark, which grows to about 6m (20ft), has acquired the reputation of a relentless man-eater, but many attacks are attributable to it mistaking humans for the seals which form the bulk of its diet. Great whites are now protected in many parts of the world, and shark tourism has become a major, often controversial industry in South Africa and Australia. Still, great whites are quite rare – here are a few of the sharks leisure divers are more likely to encounter:

Grey reef shark (*Carcharinus amblyrhynchos*): One of the most common sharks of the Indo-Pacific, it reaches about 2.5m (8ft) and can be distinguished by a black band on the outer margin of its caudal fin. Often inquisitive, it inspects divers and practises intimidation swimming (jerky, exaggerated movements) if it feels threatened. It has been known to attack divers if harassed or when wounded fish are present.

White-tipped reef shark (*Triaenodon obesus*): This shark is instantly recognisable by its prominent nostrils and white spots on its first dorsal and caudal fins. Active mainly at night, it is often spotted by divers, resting on the sandy bottom or in caverns. Although mature females can grow to 2m (6.5ft), these sharks are naturally timid and pose no real threat to divers. More dangerous is the risk of ciguatera, a tropical disease that can be contracted by eating its flesh.

Scalloped hammerhead (*Sphyrna lewini*): Although it lives from the surface down to 275m (900ft) and often congregates in huge schools, the enigmatic hammerhead is an elusive fish. Divers usually feel the need to carry out deep dives when searching for the famous schools, one of the most magnificent sights in the natural world. Growing to 4.5m (15ft), this shark is very timid and is easily alarmed by the sound of a divers breathing through their regulator. However, the larger great hammerhead (*Sphyrna mokarran*) is far bolder and potentially dangerous. The distinctive head has probably evolved to space out the fish's sensory apparatus.

Bull or Zambezi shark (*Carcharinus leucas*): This is the only confirmed man-eater which sport divers can encounter easily and often appears at shark feeding sessions in the Caribbean. Thickset and powerful, it can grow to 3.4m (11ft) and will eat practically anything. It is found along the coasts of all tropical and subtropical seas, and is the only shark to swim a very long way up into rivers and lakes.

BELOW: Close encounters with sharks belie their fierce reputation

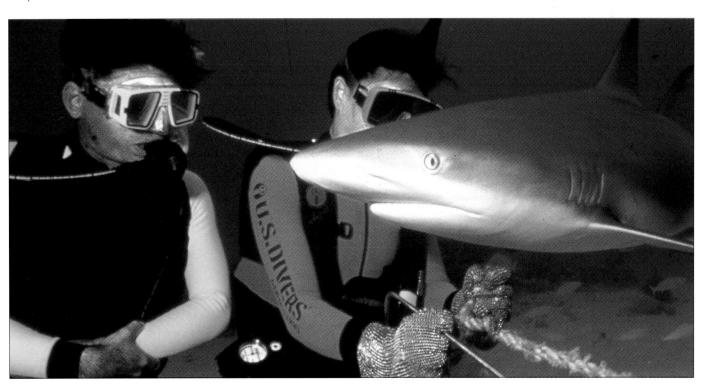

FISH TO WATCH OUT FOR:
Dangerous denizens of the deep

There is a popular saying that any marine organism slow enough to be touched by a diver probably has a defensive mechanism powerful enough to harm a human. Put simply, if you can touch it – don't. Apart from the sharks (all of which should be treated with respect), the oceans boast a dizzying array of venomous and toxic creatures which are best given a wide berth. Many of these, such as the non-aggressive sea snakes, advertise their poison with garish coloration, but other dangerous animals are harder to spot.

Scorpionfish are the major group of venomous fish that are potentially dangerous to divers. There are about 24 species of scorpionfish ranging in a variety of locations from the temperate waters of the North Atlantic to the tropical Caribbean sea. They are held responsible for about 300 cases of poisoning every year. The venom glands of these fish are linked to hollow spines in the dorsal, anal and pelvic parts of the fish's body. To compound matters, most members of this family are masters of disguise and are practically invisible to the untrained eye. The most lethal member is the reef stonefish, whose poison causes

extreme agony, and even death. Divers should never provoke any scorpionfish as they may lunge forward in self-defence with their venomous spines erect.

Some species of jellyfish pose an equally lethal threat, particularly the box jellyfish of Australia and the Pacific. Although reactions differ, extreme pain, cardiac arrest and death may result from contact with animals like Flecker's box jellyfish, the largest and most dangerous of the family. Box jellyfish are swimming advertisements for full-body wetsuits, even in areas where high water temperatures could allow skin-diving. More commonly encountered, though less dangerous, is the moon jellyfish, which has a huge range and gives thousands of swimmers skin rashes every year. Although many jellyfish have no sting, divers who choose to err on the side of caution should generally avoid them.

Colonies of stationary animals like coral and sea anemones have evolved nasty stings to discourage fish from bumping into them. Although the standard divers' code states that coral should never be touched, accidents do happen. Be careful when swimming near staghorn, elkhorn or fire coral, each of which has a sting rather stronger than the average nettle. Even sponges can pack a punch: beware the appropriately named do-not-touch-me sponge of Florida and Mexico, which inflicts immediate stinging followed by burning and blistering that can last for several days.

Beware also the beauty of the geographer cone of the Indo-Pacific, which has made it a prize for shell collectors. Cones should never be handled without heavy gloves, as they are armed with elongated radula barbs that inject a powerful neuro-toxin whenever they are manhandled. No anti-venoms are available and death from cardiac arrest is common.

When walking through shallows, it pays to shuffle one's feet through the sand rather than taking clear steps. The shuffling is sufficient to ward off bottom dwellers like scorpionfish and rays, and can reduce the possibility of getting an urchin spine deeply embedded in your foot. Thick neoprene boots are also highly recommended.

It has been estimated that less than one per cent of the world's population has had the chance to witness the fecundity of the seas at first hand. Although everyone on this planet depends on the oceans for their survival, only a privileged few can even begin to appreciate what goes on beneath the waves.

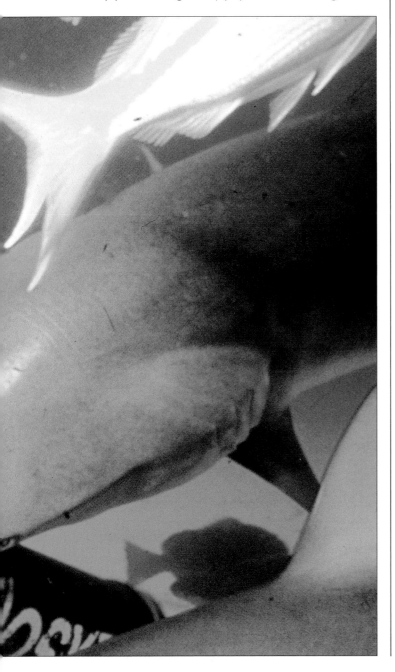

LEFT: Feeding sharks is popular in the Caribbean, but unseen dangers also lurk in these waters.

PRESERVING THE ENVIRONMENT

Scuba diving has seen several booms since Jacques Cousteau first popularised the demand valve back in the '50s, to the extent that the sport is now a mainstream activity rather than the preserve of eccentrics and explorers. But the growing numbers of dive tourists congregating at famous sites like Ras Mohammed has had a noticeable effect on the environment. Sometimes the effect is positive, as was the case when the Malaysian island of Sipadan was rescued from dynamite fishermen in the early '80s. Now, Sipadan is trying to find a way to deal with its own popularity, and tourist numbers there are being controlled in an attempt to preserve its unique environment.

Quite simply, scuba diving has become so popular that divers have to take on new responsibilities for the environments they enjoy. Gone are the days when filmmakers could crunch into as much slow growing coral as they liked in their attempts to get the perfect shot of a fish. Today, the no-touch rule is becoming more universal as diving communities begin to wake up to their environmental responsibilities.

Far greater threats come from beyond the world of leisure diving. Humans have harvested several marine creatures to extinction, and the slaughter has increased with the global population explosion and modern technologies employed by sea fisheries. The greatest impact of humans on ocean ecology is not by harvesting any one particular species, but the wholesale removal of more than 90 million tons of fish per year by the world's fishing nations. This figure represents not only the reported catch of the supermarket species, but also the unmarketable fish, mammals and birds which have the ill fortune to be landed in the same nets.

Today, the largest fishery in the world is the Alaskan walleye pollock fishery in the Bering Sea, where the annual harvest is more than 6 million tons. Recent studies have revealed that this removal of fish has had a terrible impact on the other animal populations that depend on pollock, including sea lions, fur seals and marine birds.

Another aspect of the human onslaught on the oceans is the dumping of toxic materials in both sheltered coastal waters and offshore waters, as well as the sewage that is discharged into harbours and lagoons. In some areas fish have become too contaminated for safe consumption, and enormous concentrations of deadly pollutants such as polychlorinated biphenyls (PCBs) have been detected in the tissues of whales, dolphins and other apex predators.

No one is exempt from responsibility for the preservation of the oceans, but divers are uniquely aware of the changes in the sea, and carry extra responsibility. Diving and surfing organisations in particular are becoming increasingly political as the trend towards environmental awareness gathers momentum. International organisations such as the United Nations are beginning to wake up to the serious issues surrounding the future of the oceans. But the real work of saving the sea will not be carried out in diplomatic conferences, but in the hearts and minds of ordinary people who care about the world.

LEFT: Breaching humpback whale

ABOVE: Delicate anemones need a clean environment

INDEX

Contributing editors
Graeme Gourlay, Colin Doeg, Steve Warren, Siski Green, Matt Crowther, Simon Rogerson.

Pictures
With special thanks to:
Pat Morrissey 11,12,21,33,35,47,50,51,52,53,56,65,66,68,69,72,73,74,76,77,78,80,84,85,87,88,89,91,109. Douglas Seifert
98,100,108. Steve Warren (Ocean Optics) 22,25,27,28,30,31,32,39,86,87,95. Sid Thaker (Ocean Optics) 81. Andrew Bell 62,63.
Malcolm Hey 58,59,67. T Newton 49,61. R Bull 96. Graeme Gourlay 101. The Barbados Tourist office, Unexso, Stuart Cove's Dive
South Ocean, Stella Maris Resort, The Bahamas Tourist Office, Mauritius Tourism Promotion Authority, Tourism Authority of Thailand,
Seychelles Tourist Office, Spectrum Colour Library.

Illustrations
Ian Legge, Rob Shone.